What early rea

"I read the book twice not because it gripped my attention. The intention is clear: you are brilliantly engaged. It triggers healthy introspection and self-calibration about under-developed potential. It cuts to the bone. No need to call a friend or ask the audience. The answers are within reach. Absorb, apply and practice. This book is not for sissies".

Wynand Marx, Chief Executive Officer, Bluhm, Burton Engineers, South Africa, Canada and Australia

"In *LeadingMatters*, Ian Dean reveals that competent leaders take nothing for granted, and that true learning happens through action. There are no magical secrets—just intentional effort, meaningful influence, and the courage to guide others toward shared goals. Drawing on a lifetime of global experience, Dean provides fresh insights, clear frameworks, and practical guidance for achieving personal mastery, fulfilment, and enduring impact".

Diane Ritson, Radical free thinker and "go-to" solution provider, Global

"*LeadingMatters* emerges as a groundbreaking guide, encapsulating decades of unparalleled experience and wisdom in personal and leadership development. Ian's work has profoundly influenced prestigious institutions, organisations, global environmental agencies and thousands of people. The book captures practical insights and strategies, drawing from Ian's notable legacy in enhancing personal and institutional capacity. The insights are applicable to people at every level, and they aim to foster excellence no matter age, gender, culture, profession or life phase. I wholeheartedly recommend *LeadingMatters* to anyone who has the desire and courage to make the most of their life".

Dan Amlalo, Former Executive Director, EPA Ghana

"The difference between this leadership book and all the others on the shelf is the author. The perspective on these pages comes from a man who advised leaders globally for decades. Ian Dean gets you. He gets your organization, your country, your culture, your aspirations, and your personality, and he will get you to your next goal with *LeadingMatters*".

Susan M. Moore, PhD, an individual and organizational change facilitator, USA

"*LeadingMatters* for everybody effectively conveys lifelong wisdom in the various facets for leading and leadership combined with a focus on personal competences, personal mastery, personal and skills modelling. It is an honour to promote this masterpiece to everybody. I regret not having had access to such a publication in my early career".

Professor Pieter S Steyn, Past President of the International Union of Pure and Applied Chemistry (IUPAC) retired Senior Director Research of Stellenbosch University

"*LeadingMatters* is a great reminder on so many beautiful aspects of leadership. What a glorious journey leadership is...the difficulties which we solve in the end, the crisis that present growth and opportunity to learn, refine and try harder. The joy of sharing great experiences. The rewards and gratitude in seeing team members flourish and develop. But above all the need for self-awareness and self-correction".

Valentine Nichas, Chief Executive Officer, Spur Corporation, Middle East and Africa

"Through this book and his mentorship, over many years, Ian has provided me with great insight on leadership and life. In *LeadingMatters*, Ian finally puts these important lessons in written word and describes the importance of leading as an everyday objective for everyone, "no exceptions".

Steven Mischler, Senior Research Scientist, USA

"*LeadingMatters* is fascinating, extremely well expressed and thought-provoking. It is clear that immense experience in this field throughout Ian's life has provided insights which many may think they know but which few can fully understand - let alone implement. This insightful book should be compulsory reading for all senior level school children and students so that the common mind-set of 'following' and 'acceptance' in our world may start to change. I will keep referring to *LeadingMatters* with my grandchildren"!

Cathy Raymond, Teacher, Mother and proud Grandparent, South Africa

"Ian seamlessly integrates his encyclopaedic knowledge of the vast literature on leadership with his own unique and profound insights. These come from a lifetime of studying leadership in the real world, coaching people to develop it, and pondering deeply its roots, facets and manifestations. His insights are often challenging, occasionally polemical, but always valuable".

Brian Armstrong, Director of Businesses and Professor of Digital Business, South Africa

"Wow, what a read. For the many millions who have not yet realized just how important leading is in their life from beginners to highly accomplished leaders, *LeadingMatters* is a revelation that will surprise, challenge and equip you".

Sinikinesh Beyene Jimma, Head, Marine and Freshwater Branch,
United Nations Environment Programme, Kenya

"Mr Dean is a wizard in the leadership coaching business. Do read this book. And maybe with a pen in hand. Then go back in 3 months and reflect again on what you learned ... and, more importantly, applied. Enjoy the journey"!

Dr Geoff Garrett, formerly President and CEO, CSIR, South Africa;
Chief Executive, CSIRO, Australia; Chief Scientist, Queensland

"Over three decades ago, I learned from the passion that a younger Ian Dean brought to the art of leading on leading. The older version Dean continues that passion, much like a Michelin-starred chef continues winning his stars every year. Ian brings dedication, passion, innovation, and attention to detail to his art in *LeadingMatters*.
I am challenged and enthused afresh. I hope that all who read this work are too."

Dr Ehrlich Desa, former director National Institute of Oceanography, CSIR,
India and Global Capacity Building Lead, IOC, UNESCO, France

"This book is truly a passion piece from Ian. Whether you are a new leader looking for some tips and inspiration or whether you are a seasoned leader looking for some revitalization and new purpose, this book is a must-have. Your guide to becoming your best leader yet".

Ms Marie-May Jeremie, Friend, Student and CEO of SeyCCAT, Seychelles

"Dean has crafted a compelling guide to aid your journey towards personal mastery in our crowded and turbulent world. His pragmatic conversations will help you to navigate your choices and re-craft your life-long leadership voice to get things done. An essential and honest reflective read".

David Carolus, Group CEO Dental Information Systems, South Africa

"*LeadingMatters* is a remarkable work that demystifies the concept of leadership for readers from all walks of life. Written in a simple yet engaging style, it offers examples and pondering points that bring leadership principles to life. Books on leadership can often feel dry, but Ian's ability to present complex ideas in a straightforward and impactful manner is refreshing. As I read through the chapters, it felt as though Ian was personally guiding me through the nuances of leadership. I believe *LeadingMatters* will leave a lasting impression on anyone who takes the time to read it".

Dr Vidhu A. Sane, Chief Scientist, PGEL, AcSIR-NBRI Coordinator, India

"Ian distils a lifetime of leadership development and coaching into a compact but dense volume which both challenges and encourages. It liberates leadership development from business schools and executive programs and brings it to all of us, making it accessible via visual prompts, practical suggestions and a conversational tone. This is no three quick steps to anything; it is a set of solid principles and practices to guide everyone on their leadership journey".

Wessel du Preez, Commercial Contracting Lead, UK

IAN DEAN

LeadingMatters

Austin Macauley Publishers
LONDON · CAMBRIDGE · NEW YORK · SHARJAH

Copyright © Ian Dean 2025

The right of Ian Dean to be identified as author of this work has been asserted by the author in accordance with sections 77 and 78 of the Copyright, Designs and Patents Act 1988.

All rights reserved. No part of this publication may be reproduced, stored in a retrieval system, or transmitted in any form or by any means, electronic, mechanical, photocopying, recording, or otherwise, without the prior permission of the publishers.

Any person who commits any unauthorised act in relation to this publication may be liable to criminal prosecution and civil claims for damages.

The story, the experiences, and the words are the author's alone.

A CIP catalogue record for this title is available from the British Library.

ISBN 9781035869589 (Paperback)
ISBN 9781035869596 (ePub e-book)

www.austinmacauley.com

First Published 2025

Austin Macauley Publishers Ltd®
1 Canada Square
Canary Wharf
London
E14 5AA

*For my son, Adrian,
and daughter Marisa.*

Contents

Awakening 13
When the Obvious Is Crucial but Not Obvious 16
When Dangerous Becomes Disastrous 19
What Does It Take to Lead? 20
Mind the Gap 25
Waypoint 1: A Call to Action 29
A Checklist for Leading and Leadership 33
    Start with a Fun Test 33
    Suggested answers 40
    Leading Explained 42
    Leadership Defined 51
    Influence that comes with Positional Authority 56
    Influence that comes with Personal Authority 59
    Other Influencers: Seduction, Fear, Manipulation and Intimidation 64
    The Gold Standard of Trust 65
    The Role of Competence in Leadership 70
    Did You Play Your Twiddly Bits? 77
    What About Proficiency? 80
    Crafting Your Competence Framework 83
Our Functional Competences 93
    Work as Meaning and Identity 93
    Chinese Rice Farmers Versus SpaceX Engineers 95
Our Personal Competences 97
    Deciding What Matters Most 97
    Personal Mastery as a Cornerstone for Leading and Life 97
    Personal Mastery Unpacked 99
    Why Is Personal Mastery So Important 101
    Key Features of Mindsets 102
    Mindsets on the Move: Evolving Paradigms and Mental Models 104
    The Leverage for Change 106
    Personal Modelling 106
    Behaviour and Skills Modelling 109

    Values and Attitudes: No Easy Matter 118
    Easy Words: Tough Realities 122
    Habits and Routines: Elevators Up – Greasy Poles Down.................124
    What Experience Teaches: The Cecil Atherstone Story 129
    Who Am 'I'? The Rocky Road to Identity 133
    Is 'I' a Fixed Point? Who's to Tell? 135

Waypoint 2: A Call to Action 138

Leadership Work...140

Awareness 142
    Analytical Tools 146

Responses 149
    The Holy Grail of Leadership..150
    Decision Criteria for Response Selection..158

Resourcing 159
    Four Resourcing Routines...160

Partnering 163
    Co-creating Conditions Wherein People Can Excel 167
    Securing Understanding and Acceptance..169

Delivery 171

Learning...172

At What Point Is a Person Competent to Lead?...................................180

A Vocabulary for Leading and Leadership...183

Waypoint 3: Moving Forward: Next Steps 188
    Getting to Carnegie Hall 188

Recommended Resources for Further Development 191
    Understanding and Enjoying Life 191
    Learning: The Greatest Means to Abundant Ends...........................192
    Leading and Leadership..193
    Films and documentaries 194

Thanks 195

Index..198

Author's Information 200

You, colleagues, family, friends, strangers, celebrities, parents, high achievers, scholars, stragglers, me and all the rest.

Wealthy or Poor

Male or Female

Every occupation
Retired
Unemployed

LeadingMatters to everybody. No exceptions.

All races, genders, creeds, cultures and countries

Introvert or Extrovert

Teenagers to 100+ years old

"Our ability or inability to lead influences the outcomes of close to everything we achieve or fail to achieve."

Succeeding
Raising kids
Lasting relationships
Wealth creation
Resolving conflict
Kicking substance abuse
Falling in love
Graduating
Career building
Winning almost anything
Being you

AWAKENING

It's 8 after 8. It's been a long day. A day of writing. A week of writing. One of many weeks over many months. In truth, over twenty years because that's how long this LeadingMatters quest has been germinating in me.

Earlier versions were refined, rewritten, repositioned and re-everything to find a warm responsive connection with you the reader. I tried my best. I desperately want to convey messages of value. Messages that share insights and experiences you can adapt and use as best suits your circumstances.

This evening, while walking Charlie, our miniature Schnauzer, I realised with considerable shock that the two most essential lessons of my life, the two I had shared with such passion around the world for so many years, were missing from the start.

I had tried, as I was writing, to be politically correct. Gender neutral. Considerate of what prospective readers might want. Mindful of how I might need to bend to secure an agent and a publisher. At least somewhat respectful of the screeds of hubris churned out annually as new, novel and groundbreaking unlocked secrets on leading and leadership – which of course is rarely true.

As much as I care about these things, I realised I had to move on. I had become defensive and preoccupied with awakening what might be, instead of dealing with what is. No following of readers. "Tough, Ian Dean. Deal with it. No agents or publishers. Tough. Deal with it. No hugs and cheers from my family and friends. Tough. Deal with it."

Two essential lessons. If you want to live a full life, as indeed, we all should:

- We must find and speak in our own voice and
- We must deal with whatever comes at us, as a consequence of who we choose to be.

There it was, right before my eyes. A lifetime of insight hidden from view by the pressures of the day. How? Why? So much of life is there before us to be savoured and enjoyed to the benefit of all. Yet we forget or miss those insights and opportunities in the heat of many moments.

David Whyte in *Crossing the Unknown Sea* wrote: "A life's work is not a series of stepping stones onto which we calmly place our feet, but more like an ocean crossing where there is no path, only a heading, a direction, which, of itself, is in conversation with the elements. Looking back for a sense of reference, we see the wake we have left as only a brief, glimmering trace on the waters."

In reality, we all leave more than a brief, glimmering trace in life. We are a part of what has gone before us and what we leave will become a part of those who follow. Our choices and our voice will make a difference – of that, there can be no doubt. What that difference can be, and how we make it, is the focus of this book.

Right Before Our Eyes

WHEN THE OBVIOUS IS CRUCIAL BUT NOT OBVIOUS

Can the obvious be so obvious that it is no longer obvious? Something that becomes so everyday that we no longer think about it? A single part so seemingly insignificant in the larger scheme of life, that it goes unnoticed, like an O-ring.

An O-ring? On 28 January 1986, the space shuttle Challenger broke apart 73 seconds into its flight, killing all seven crew members aboard. It was caused by an O-ring seal failure. One component out of thousands of components.

We are all exposed to the risks of O-ring failures in our life. The little things we overlook, take for granted and ignore. The little but crucial things that can cause us great loss. One such component is when convention becomes so every day that we no longer think about its continued relevance and validity.

Convention links leading to leaders and leadership. That applies, correctly so, to a small percentage of any population. What about the majority of people who are not designated as leaders? Is leading not relevant to them? If you believe that, it would be like saying, "Only chefs cook."

Leading is an essential life skill for every person on the planet. Every person. No exceptions. That includes the hapless, homeless Jim and Julie sleeping on a park bench in the Washington, DC Metro area, and their fellow strugglers exposed to poverty in

Africa, Europe, South America, Asia and just about everywhere else in the world.

Leading is not captive to institutions, organisations and businesses that include it in formally defined roles. Definitely not.

Millions of job holders such as doctors, architects, designers, politicians, lawyers, judges, researchers, publishers, journalists, artisans, journeymen, carpenters, accountants, sales associates, caterers, teachers and academics rarely regard leading as a crucial aspect of what they do. They may argue differently, but they are wrong.

Leading is just as important to the many constituencies of people who live and function without titles, ranks, formal prescriptions and neatly defined jobs. That's the world of parents, artists, the retired, the unemployed, scholars, writers, students and other young people.

Life does not stop when people retire, go through menopause (male or female) or join the ranks of the elderly. It doesn't end when we lose our way. On the contrary. That's exactly when we need to reach deeply into ourselves to allow our positive actions to overcome our misfortunes.

Nor does life start with puberty or some invisible permission granted by complex, often outdated, cultures and the institutions that seek to define it. Life, real life, not merely existence, starts when we acquire the capacity to engage on an equal footing, the structures, institutions, models, belief systems, people and powers that, both directly and indirectly, shape our identity and our choices.

For that transition, which many regard as the journey of a lifetime, leading plays a pivotal role. Not only our capacity to lead but in very significant ways, the leading we are exposed to from others. Our formative years are lived in containers designed, built and imposed upon us by others.

We learn about the world through the eyes of others. Their beliefs. Their choices. Their teaching. Their fears. Their leading. We absorb and comply. During those early years, we have not yet developed the cognitive capacity to filter and evaluate what is handed down. We reside in the great lake of 'The-Way-It-Is'.

That's where significant percentages of people continue to live out their life. Tragically so. To emerge from that lake we must awaken to our own understanding of the way it is, not as an entirely different or opposing narrative, but as a blending of relevance and truth. It's a life-long journey of adaptation and adjustment. A process of unlearning and relearning.

It's a massive responsibility to recognise how what we hand down through our leading impacts the lives of others. And, crucially, how we continue to be influenced throughout our lives by the leading provided by others.

> *The scars of the fights we never had are the most painful.*
>
> *Not stupid fights for no reason other than anger and self-interest.*
>
> *The fights avoided by doing nothing when action was needed.*
>
> *Our failure to stand up against injustice, discrimination, false doctrines and evil.*
>
> *Our reluctance to reimagine ourselves through each phase of life.*

WHEN DANGEROUS BECOMES DISASTROUS

You arrive at the scene of an accident on a busy highway. A delivery vehicle has skidded, hit the safety barrier and overturned. The driver and crew are trapped and calling for help. There is fuel everywhere. Onlookers are milling around in confusion and shock. Oncoming traffic remains heavy, without slowing. The situation is, to say the least, dangerous.

There are no paramedics, traffic officers or people with crisis-handling experience who can step up and take charge of the situation. No persons with designations that include any responsibilities to lead. Nothing is happening. Dangerous moves to disastrous in the blink of an eye.

I expect you think I'm going to say: "Leadership is missing." That in part is true. More crucial though is the willingness of so many people to be passive onlookers in situations that demand action. At work, at home and in the playground of life, they are passive onlookers of the wonderment that remains untapped in themselves – and in others. Forgetful of the difference they can make and the legacy they will leave. That's when life, yours, mine and the trapped crew, comes to a standstill.

WHAT DOES IT TAKE TO LEAD?

Failing to recognise leading as a life skill is one thing. Failing to appreciate the time and effort required to lead with impact, is a bigger problem.

Sixty hours of instruction are required to learn the basics of flying a single-engine aircraft. It takes hundreds of hours of further, often gruelling, training to fly more complex equipment and pass annual simulator tests for recertification.

No spin. No spam.

The many years and often the lifetime it takes for professionals to achieve functional mastery is well known. People in the arts, education, academia, sport, trades, hospitality, armed forces and many, many more areas are very familiar with the long hours of study, sacrifice and practice needed to qualify. Even our early education can consume up to twelve years, and so it goes.

Considering the importance of leading – what we provide and what we receive, would it be unreasonable to expect people from every walk of life, irrespective of any support that may be forthcoming from employers, education systems and broader society – to invest in building their expertise? Certainly many do. Most don't. Just ask your family and friends should you have any doubts.

This void is not difficult to understand. Leading was and still is not regarded as a critical life skill – one that everybody should be nurtured throughout their life. It has been my experience, and I believe very strongly that the low awareness can be attributed to outdated educational systems across the globe, coupled with serious gaps in curiosity and expanded learning in adulthood. Far too many people simply don't appreciate the significance of leading in their life and even where they do, what exactly they can do about it.

To lead requires learning to lead. There is no such thing as 'natural leaders' or so-called 'born leaders'. Leaders are made by conscious choice – a choice we all should make.

Diagram 1: How leading influences who we become

Your LeadingMatters

The manner in which you lead and how the leading of others impacts you

influences

The choices you make and the actions you take regarding your development and identity impacts

influences

What Does It Take to Lead?

All human endeavour and achievement, with very few exceptions, flows from *aspiration* and mastery of the *fundamentals*.

In a well-worth-reading publication, *The Tipping Point: How Little Things Can Make a Big Difference,* Malcolm Gladwell, presents the idea of 10,000 hours as a milestone in relation to achieving expertise and mastery in a particular field. He suggests that it takes approximately 10,000 hours of deliberate practice to achieve high-level proficiency in any complex skill.

There is no hard science to confirm whether Gladwell is right or wrong. What I do know is that it takes hundreds of hours with repeated practice to master the fundamentals of leading, and a lifetime of practice to achieve consistently high impact.

A small word of caution may be valuable here. The domain of leading is dominated by media and resources, not exclusively, but primarily targeted and tailored for the business world. That is hardly surprising given the annual multi-billion dollar global spend on leader capacity development in business.

Markets of that size attract suppliers and competition on a mega scale. The claims, the hype, the exaggerated differentiation, along with 'revealed' secrets and one-size-fits-all offerings have introduced mind-blowing hubris. Seductive narratives about authenticity, courage, secrets for a successful life, principle-centric approaches, leading with soul, servant-centred winning traits, behavioural show-stoppers, transactional formulas and transformational and assured hero status all provide strong emotional appeal. The icing and the candles have become the cake.

Mastering the fundamentals of leading requires that you actually get to the fundamentals and not the window dressing. There are no secrets and no shortcuts. There is no single approach to leading that is suitable for all situations, people or challenges. When you hear or read such claims, know for sure it's all smoke and mirrors.

The filters and amplifiers you use to shape your identity and curate your development are a matter of personal choice and judgement. Leading is not a science. There are no universal models for easy plug and play.

In a connected way, Christine Kennelly, an award-winning journalist wrote in *The Invisible History of the Human Race*, "We are all creatures of changeless truths and interesting possibilities. Once you are born, your spot in the tree of humanity is fixed. You will always have emerged out of everything that shaped the tree before you – the biology and the history." She continues: "As you develop and grow older in whatever world you live in, the calculations change. Your family, the history of your community, your government, and even your food alter them. You alter them."

Gabor Maté maintains that children are never born to the same parents. Time changes them. The context changes. The children enter the world at different times and experience different conditions.

What's your personal view on the what, why and how of leading? Be assured that the obvious is not so obvious. Invite a few colleagues and family members to share their perspectives on:

- What does it mean to lead?

- Who should be able to lead?

- What are the fundamentals of leading?

klaw tsrif tsum uoy nur ot

lwarc tsrif tsum ouy klaw ot

tuo erutnev dna ksir tsum uoy lwarc ot

Curiosity opens discovery

Discovery opens our world.

MIND THE GAP

Londoners and visitors to London know the famous London Underground announcement well: 'Mind the gap'. It can be seen as a call for action, a reminder that a bigger step is needed to avoid the gap between coach and platform.

Gaps are interesting phenomena in life. Mind the gap between what is possible and desirable and what actually exists. Mind the gap between what is preached and what is practised. Mind the gap between what we think we know and what we actually know.

Try this quick assignment to experience the point.

Firstly, rate the importance you attach to thinking skills on a

10-point scale, where 10 is super important, 5 is average and 1 relegates thinking skills to irrelevance. Select any number in the range 1 to 10 and record it.

When I have applied this assignment with hundreds of people over the years, the overwhelming response is 10. Then I ask the responders to give a spontaneous, informal five to ten-minute chat on thinking skills. Tell us what they are, how they are developed and how much time they spend trying to improve them. Or do they think they have already reached their optimum level of thinking? Try it yourself.

Whether in India, Mexico, Ghana, the USA, Singapore or Kenya, the results are the same. The majority of people, no matter what their background or qualifications, really struggle to explain their thinking skills. A minute or two describing types of thinking such as analytical, problem-solving, conceptual and deductive reasoning are standard responses. Little to no mention is made of the actual skills such as perception and pattern recognition, memory recall, reasoning, the creation and application of new models, the role of intelligence and the benefit of smiling, sleep and diet in maintaining healthy cognitive functioning.

Despite thinking being so important, 10 on a 10-point scale, thinking, like love, leading, learning and other life skills, is taken for granted on the flawed notion that somehow, 'we know'. A weekend at a Student Council Member Camp, a short course or two here and there and some reading with trial and error learning, are frequently seen as sufficient foundations for important life skills. Sorry. That is incorrect.

As long as we:

- Fail to recognise the importance of leading in our personal life, irrespective of explicitly assigned responsibilities to lead;

- Invest little to no time and energy in nurturing our capacity to lead as a life-long undertaking;

- Overlook the difference between what we think we know, what we actually know and what we are able to do with what we know, there will be gaps in our make-up where none should exist.

O-rings. Plural. Many of them.

Diagram 2: When what we think we know isn't so – Advertisement for the Olympic and Titanic cruise liners

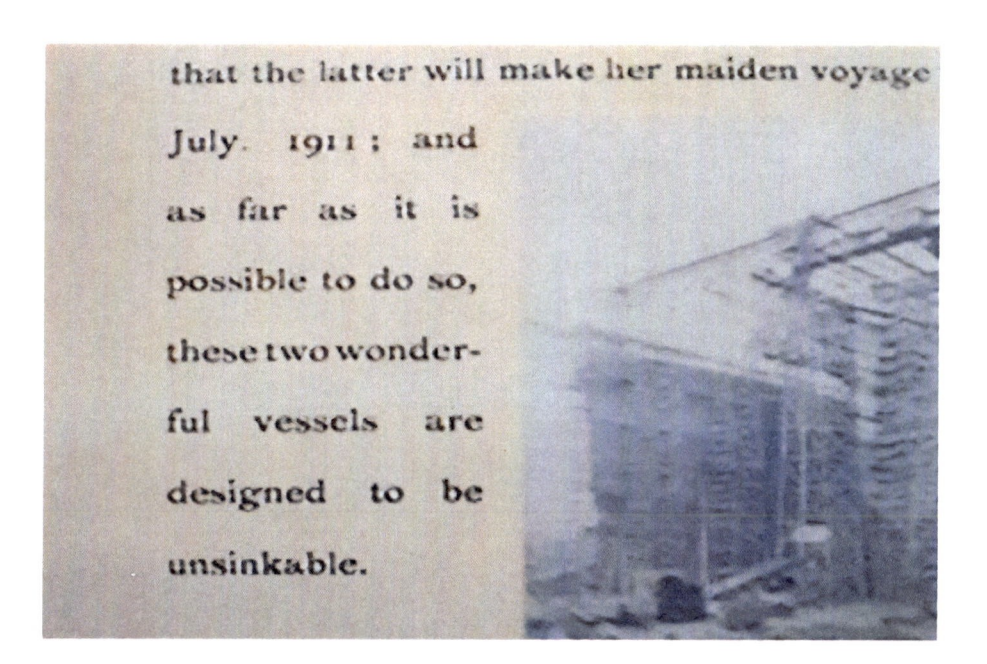

> that the latter will make her maiden voyage July. 1911; and as far as it is possible to do so, these two wonderful vessels are designed to be unsinkable.

- "There is no reason anyone would want to use a picture messaging service when they can just send a text," Mark Zuckerberg, in 2012.

- In 1966, *Time* magazine ran a bold prediction: "Remote shopping, while entirely feasible, will flop."

- "640K ought to be enough for anybody," Bill Gates, in 1981.

- Harvard Professor Robert Metcalf, founder of 3Com Digital, predicted in 1995 that the internet would "soon go spectacularly supernova and in 1996 catastrophically collapse."

IN SUMMARY: POINTS TO PONDER

1.
*Leading is an essential life skill for everybody. No exceptions.
It's rarely recognized as such.*

2.
*Clarity on what it means to lead has become buried
in hype, inflated claims, heroics and turf wars.*

3.
Leading others and leading self are two sides of the same coin.

4.
Without leadership everything comes to a grinding halt.

5.
*That's not a welcome experience when, like oxygen,
your life depends on it – as it always does.*

6.
*Leading is achieved through influence, whether
consequential and/or intentional.*

7.
Leading is a means to an end, not an end in itself.

8.
*Becoming a hero or celebrity are not outcomes pursued
by people who truly understand what it means to lead.*

9.
*Who we are, what we choose and what we stand up
for or fail to do in this regard, are our 24/7/52/lifetime
actions for leading self and influencing others.*

WAYPOINT 1: A CALL TO ACTION

Dear Reader,

The fact that many captains of commercial airliners have four bars on their shoulder lapel, 20,000 plus flying hours logged, and a few greying hairs, does not exempt them from having to complete a long list of checks to ensure their aircraft's readiness and safety for flight. Pre-flight Inspection; Cockpit Preparation; Flight Controls Check; Systems Check; FMS (Flight Management System) Programming: The captain enters the flight plan, waypoints, and other relevant data into the aircraft's FMS to ensure accurate navigation during the flight.

The discipline is strictly followed, as the co-pilot sits alongside, and checks the captain checking! These are experienced professionals following systemised routines from a defined checklist – a checklist they could complete in their sleep.

Competent people take nothing for granted. They calibrate where they are relative to their plans. They repeat the step at each waypoint until they reach their destination. Then they start again because we all have many destinations to reach in life.

'Waypoints': Co-ordinates we expect to reach by a certain time; a point at which we must make important decisions about the next phase of our journey. What a fantastic concept. That should also be a regular routine whenever we read a non-fiction book such as this. What do we want to discover and how will we know we have? How should we proceed? The potential value that a good book offers does not accrue automatically.

Several years ago, a close friend who lives and works in London, sent an email in which he enquired whether I had read the book, *The Art of Thinking Clearly* by Rolf Dobelli. I had not. I purchased a copy and read it cover to cover. Dobelli lists a series of cognitive biases and simple errors we all make in our day-to-day thinking. The blurb on the rear cover refers to *The Secrets of Perfect Decision-Making*. I'm not sure about the 'secrets' part, but it offers amazing lessons and is a very worthwhile read.

Two months later I asked my friend the following:

- "How many thinking errors does Dobelli list in his book?"

- "Of those, how many could he name?"

- "Of those, how many had he applied to eliminate errors from his thinking to improve his decision-making?"

He replied, "50, 12, 3." For the record, Dobelli lists 99 errors. More than 12 are worth remembering by name, and we would all benefit from applying at least 14 to 15.

We read fine books. We attend excellent lectures and talks. Events and circumstances expose us to valuable experiences. What benefit do we get when we are unable to recall them? More importantly, apply them? Planting without enjoying the fruits of your labour can hardly be a satisfying experience. There is no prescription nor presumption here.

Just a serious challenge.

You have reached a waypoint in this book. A case has been made for leading as an essential life skill for all. No exceptions. Whether we hold formal leadership responsibilities or simply need to lead because of our circumstances. You either agree or you disagree, and your decision should determine how you want to proceed.

One of the five lessons Apple's co-founder Steve Jobs shared during the Commencement Speech delivered at Stanford University was: 'Stay hungry, stay foolish'. I hope the richness of what he shared will help your decision-making.

How do you plan to proceed?

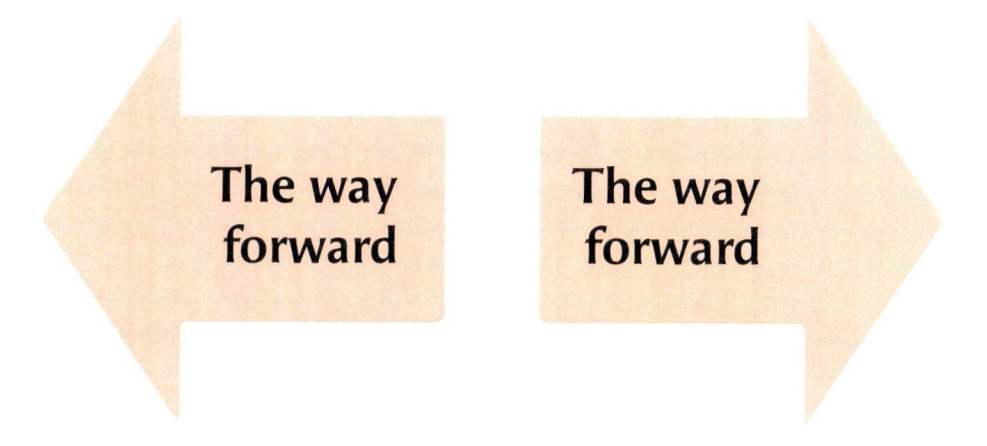

⬅ **The way forward**   **The way forward** ➡

Some options for moving forward

Reader	Where am I?	Possible next steps
A-League	I'm a seasoned campaigner – experienced leader – already a best of the best role model – part of the converted.	Quick self-check/update. Remove the weeds. Refresh my destination – A life equipped to deal with life. Or, I know it all. Abort – find something else to do.
B-League	I'm on board but short of where I can and should be. I'm aspirational and looking for ways to upskill to the A-League.	Continue reading. Complete the exercises. Practice recall. Complete the behavioural simulations. Practice. Explore the resources. Engage at every level. Persevere.
C-League	I don't get it but would like to at least understand more fully before making a decision about the way forward.	Carefully re-read pages 16 to 18. Make a few notes and reflect on the insights. Get it. Move up to the B-League. If not, proceed anyway. The dots will connect.
D-League	I recognise the merits but am content with what I have. No sincere interest in engaging at a higher level.	Being content is fine. Stopping short of exploring, enjoying and sharing your full value is not fine. Check out the options for the C-Leaguers.
The Dugout	I'm confused. Sometimes I play. Sometimes I don't.	Confusion is not a terminal disease. If you want to play, choose the C-League. Re-ignite your aspirations.
Bystander	Life sucks. The ideas in this book suck. The people around me suck. I suck. I really don't give a s**t.	Don't bluff yourself. Fortunately, it's never too late for a person to restock their mind and empty their bowel. Check out the options for the C-Leaguers.

A CHECKLIST FOR LEADING AND LEADERSHIP

Start with a Fun Test

Here are 20 questions you can use as a dipstick test of your current understanding of leading and leadership. The intention is to provoke your thinking. There are no formula-driven answers. Leading and leadership are not scientific endeavours. An approach successfully applied today, could be disastrous tomorrow.

Please engage with the questions as they hopefully engage you. My responses to the issues the questions raise are woven into the sections that follow.

Select what you regard as the most appropriate answer:

1. A reasonably close friend of yours is quite temperamental and prone to occasional outbursts of rage. How do you respond when he/she throws a tantrum?

    a. Ignore it.

    b. Sympathise with him/her about the validity of their anger.

    c. Suggest to them that it's time they went for counselling.

    d. Ask whether they are aware of the negative impact their behaviour has.

    e. None of these.

2. Which of the following statements best defines leadership for you:
   a. Leadership is the art of knowing what must be done, by whom and by when.
   b. Leadership is the discipline of defining goals and ensuring that they are achieved.
   c. Leadership is the actions taken to achieve results through the efforts of other people.
   d. Leadership is the process of persuading people to align with policies, procedures and goals.
   e. None of these.

3. It is widely believed that one of the primary contributions leaders make to society is that they motivate people. Alternative views suggest that:
   a. One person cannot motivate another person.
   b. It's not the job of leaders to motivate other people.
   c. Motivation is a myth.
   d. None of these are valid.
   e. All of these are valid.

4. Leading and leadership are:
   a. One and the same thing.
   b. Subsets of the science of management.
   c. Natural skills that develop automatically over time.
   d. Expressions of a person's value system.
   e. None of these.

5. Influencing people is:
   a. Never easy.
   b. Dependent on power.
   c. Best achieved by using threats that evoke fear.
   d. Not possible where there are divergent value systems.
   e. Not something responsible people attempt.

6. In leadership, people who cannot think strategically:
   a. Should avoid trying to provide leadership.
   b. Defer to the people who can and do think strategically.
   c. Complete a course on strategic thinking.
   d. Recognise that strategic thinking is not a prerequisite for leading.
   e. All of these.

7. The personal characteristic or quality most mentioned by effective leaders in research is:
   a. Persistence.
   b. Desire to learn.
   c. Charisma.
   d. Intelligence.
   e. Trustworthiness.

8. The manner and style in which a person chooses to lead should ideally be:
   a. The sole prerogative of the leader.
   b. Shared between the leader and followers.
   c. Irrelevant.
   d. Left to emerge randomly over time.
   e. Flexible and contextually based.

9. People can be influenced by:
    a. Coercion.
    b. Manipulation.
    c. Persuasion.
    d. Policies and procedures.
    e. All of these.

10. An important test and manifestation of a leader's maturity is their ability to:
    a. Keep promises.
    b. Exercise courage, be considerate of others and learn to deal with everything that may occur.
    c. Ensure that people believe in themselves.
    d. Rearrange language patterns and use visual imagery.
    e. Work under pressure without losing control.
    f. Interpret all complex situations and influence people to respond to them appropriately.

11. During their formative years, young people – teenagers, adolescents and young adults should primarily focus on:
    a. Having fun without taking life too seriously.
    b. Acquiring technical/professional competence.
    c. Nurturing their capacity to lead.
    d. Understanding human nature and how it shapes identity,
    e. Making money to achieve financial independence as quickly as possible.

12. Achieving enduring happiness and sustainable success in life depends mostly on:
    a. Secure sexual relationships.
    b. Being a high achiever.
    c. Remaining open-minded with learning and adjustment.
    d. Establishing complete independence.
    e. Intellectual brilliance.

13. In order to develop their capacity to lead effectively, people must:
    a. Give up their past beliefs, values and principles.
    b. Communicate their hopes for the future.
    c. Accept the views of other people.
    d. Have a clear identity and strong self-purpose.
    e. Go for counselling.

14. A person in a senior leadership position who courageously promotes his/her views, demands loyalty and is dismissive of people who challenge long-standing traditions, should be:
    a. Admired for their leadership skills.
    b. Respected for their strength of character.
    c. a. and b.
    d. Treated with caution.
    e. Ignored.

15. There is a huge diversity of thought on what constitutes a meaningful life. There are many possibilities including inter alia, (i) high quality of life – aesthetics, (ii) achieving a high standard of living – economics, (iii) having freedom of choice, (iv) discovering self, (v) serving God(s) and (vi) contributing to humanity. When it comes to leading and leadership, the issue of a meaningful life:

    a. Has nothing to do with any leader, and they should steer clear of conversations on the subject.
    b. Should be discussed openly to reach some level of common agreement.
    c. Is a spiritual matter which is strictly private to each person.
    d. Something that belongs in the realms of psychology and not leadership.
    e. Offers a glimpse of what people regard as important and therefore insight into their choices and priorities.

16. Morality and ethics in leadership:

    a. Are a sure-fire formula for success.
    b. Suggest spiritual or religious overtones.
    c. Are a waste of time.
    d. Require personal denial.
    e. None of these.

17. A person striving to provide leadership, should:

    a. Never make promises they don't intend keeping.
    b. Consider promises as a measure of integrity.
    c. a. and b.
    d. Avoid making promises.
    e. Make promises to get results and support.

18. People can change their behaviour but not their values:
    a. No, it's the other way around.
    b. People can't change either – their values or behaviour.
    c. Once established, there is no need for people to change their values and behaviour.
    d. It's very wrong for people to change their values.
    e. None of these.

19. AI software (Artificial Intelligence) will greatly reduce the need for leading and leadership because:
    a. It will generate more comprehensive and reliable responses to complex problems than humans can.
    b. The age-old tradition of hero leaders providing all the answers is in rapid decline.
    c. Systems can be developed to replace emotions, trust and relationships that are so central to high-impact leadership.
    d. They eliminate biases and prejudice.
    e. I really don't know the answer.

20. People don't intentionally set out to fail, yet almost everybody does from time to time. The gap between well-intended actions and actual results achieved can largely be attributed to:
    a. People frequently overestimating what they are capable of achieving.
    b. People frequently underestimating the time required to complete tasks/projects – especially complex ones.
    c. A failure to recognise the gaps between what they say they cherish, and value, and the inconsistency of their actions, and behaviours in applying what they value.
    d. The universal pressure to achieve causes people to be fearful of saying 'no' to imposed deadlines and/or being perceived as uncommitted.
    e. a. and b.

Suggested answers

1. d	11. b
2. c	12. c
3. b	13. d
4. e	14. d
5. b	15. e
6. d	16. e
7. b	17. c
8. e	18. e
9. e	19. e
10. a	20. c

What is the relevance of this test? Surely not just the result you achieved and the insight it provides. The test is the tip of a larger body of knowledge and expertise that should be the subject of ongoing discussions.

Conversations between family members, students and colleagues in staff rooms and on shop floors. Deliberations in Executive offices, caucus rooms and labour unions. All over. Everyone.

How does our leading and leadership impact on others? What effect do they have on us? What pushes us away? What draws us in? How will we ever know unless we test our understanding? And that is what sharp tests should do: serve as trigger points for viral discussions.

Lest there be any doubt, the purpose of this book is to:

1. *Provide guidelines to support your personal development, irrespective of where you are at in life.*

2. *Present a compelling case for leading and leadership as essential life skills for everyone.*

3. *Provide ideas, suggestions, frameworks, and resources to craft, and renew your capacity to lead with relevance and impact.*

4. *Offer fresh insights on how Personal Mastery provides a cornerstone for discovering and enjoying deep fulfilment in life.*

Leading Explained

Let's get straight to the point. Before leading comes following. That's the default mode for all of us at birth. Nobody escapes. We are born into 'following' and, for a very unlucky number, that will be their narrow gauge rail track for life. A form of modern-day slavery with mental chains.

From our first gasp of air, we are totally dependent on those around us for survival. From that moment, we learn about ourselves and life through the 'eyes of others' – family, teachers and friends.

Their models, routines, beliefs, prejudices, expectations and behaviours become our points of reference. We learn to obey, comply and follow. Our view of the world is shaped by their view.

> *Children learn what they live.*
> – DOROTHY LAW NOLTE

The sources we are exposed to during this phase are very much a matter of chance and luck. We may be surrounded by people – parents and others, who share constructive, adaptive models of life focussed on unlocking our potential. Conversely, we could have the misfortune of being in a suppressive, controlling environment that seeks to hard-wire us into submission, and compliance without the freedom to make our own determinations.

Consider the reality of the situation. If, for some reason as a baby, we are shepherded away to a different home, different parents, in a different country with a different culture, we would eventually adopt an entirely different way of life. Our image of self, how we dress, our dietary habits, what we believe and how we live, will all be entirely different.

None of this is encoded in our DNA. It is learnt, which by implication, means it can be unlearnt where necessary, and replaced with new thinking and behaviour. This is where the leading we introduce into our life plays a vital role, and why developing an ability to lead matters so much.

As we are allowed, hopefully, to form our own views, determine our own priorities, make our own decisions and think independently, the centre of control for our lives shifts from others – externally – to us – internally. This is not an either-or process. We move to a state of mutual interdependence where we remain open to external influences while retaining the right to decide the implications for ourselves.

External influences will always be present. By adding and accepting our right to choose our identity and what we believe, we establish our unique presence in the world. As modest as it may seem, this is one of the most important development steps we will ever take. The next is learning how to give expression to who we are and what we wish to stand for. We need to develop our own voice in a crowded world where we move from following and passive response to active engaging and influence.

That requires learning to lead.

To lead: to influence both ourselves and others – to have an impact because of what we advocate and do. The words 'lead' and 'leading' have attracted many interpretations and uses over the centuries. The most common are shown in Diagrams 3, 4 and 5 on the following pages.

We can lead indirectly, that is, influence people without any intent to do so merely by the example we set. Our actions may have a positive and/or negative impact depending on how they are perceived.

We can lead with intent based on actions we take to directly influence ourselves and others. For example, we intentionally pursue life-long learning as a commitment to personal growth and renewal. We intentionally refuse to just go with the flow of life. We intentionally stand up to injustice, prejudice and evil. We establish a presence and use that presence to make a difference, hopefully positive, although it may not necessarily be.

Diagram 3: Multiple interpretations of leading

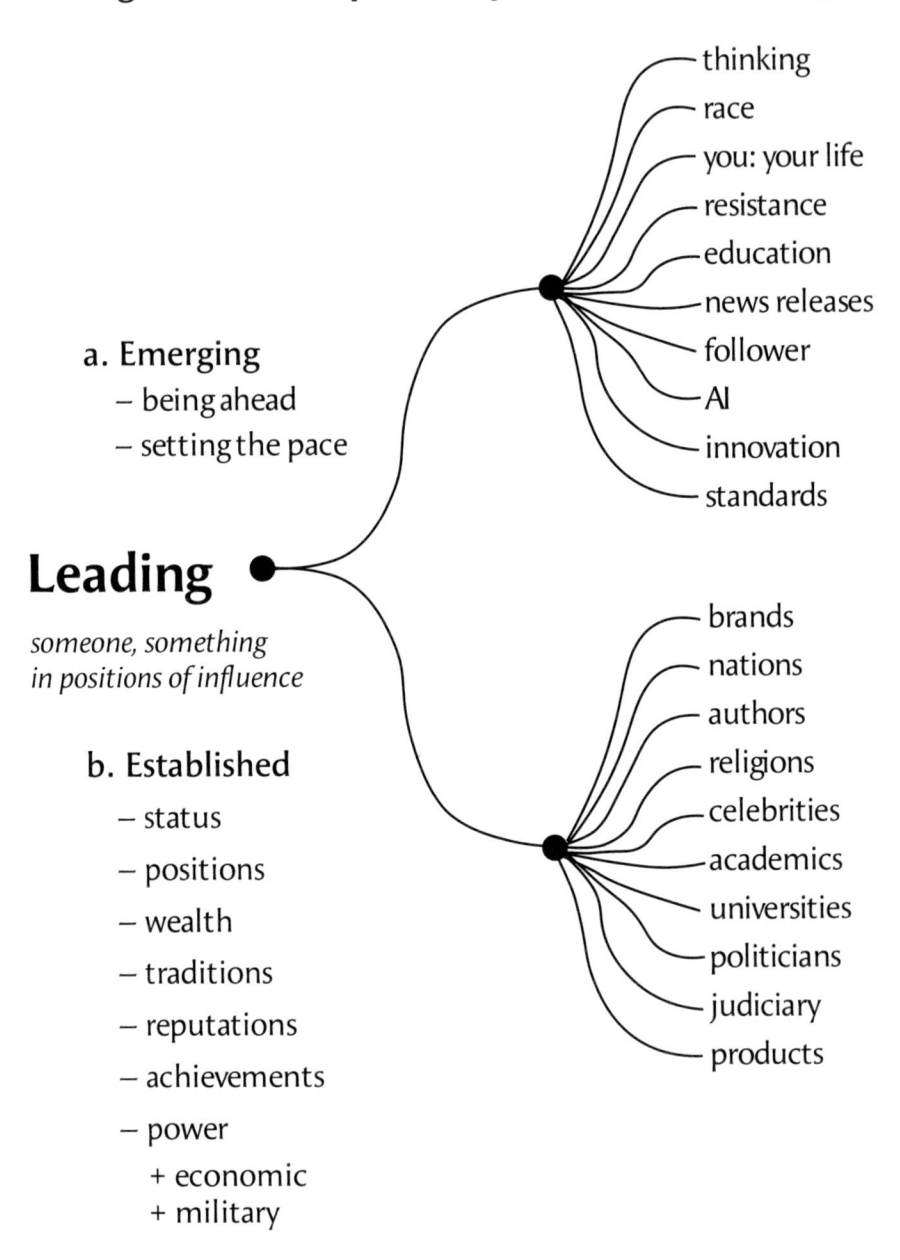

Leading

someone, something in positions of influence

a. Emerging
  – being ahead
  – setting the pace

- thinking
- race
- you: your life
- resistance
- education
- news releases
- follower
- AI
- innovation
- standards

b. Established
  – status
  – positions
  – wealth
  – traditions
  – reputations
  – achievements
  – power
    + economic
    + military

- brands
- nations
- authors
- religions
- celebrities
- academics
- universities
- politicians
- judiciary
- products

Our intent to lead – to influence, can be directed at others. For example, the impact we are looking for could be improved performance on their part, their support, their vote, their involvement and an unending list of possibilities both expansive and/or restrictive.

Humanity has grown to respect and value leaders. Leading has and continues to play a pivotal role in orderly development, the sustainability of life on Planet Earth and the co-existence of nations despite territorial conflicts. Kings, queens, emperors, presidents, prime ministers and the wealthy and highly acclaimed continue to enjoy, whether deserved or not, considerable power to influence.

There is also a shadow side to leading where people and institutions abuse their positions, and power to influence. They champion causes, doctrines or actions, which at first sight, may appear honourable or justified. In reality, they are frequently self-serving, expedient and destructive. The dogmas followed by radical right-wing elements in Christianity, Islam, Judaism, Hinduism and Roman Catholicism are examples of sub-constituencies that abuse their positions of power to subjugate people to the God(s) they claim to represent.

Fortunately, there are enlightened leaders in those religions who have not succumbed to the evils of such suffocating extremism.

The same abuses are common features in radicalised political, and terrorist organisations. They use public platforms to undermine the institutions of law and order while simultaneously fuelling fear and dissent.

The capacity to influence – to lead, whether in the hands of powerful individuals, governments, institutions, organisations, movements or organised crime in pursuit of their goals and ideals is more than just a dangerous weapon. By exploiting self-serving interpretations of what it means to obey, comply, conform, fear, submit, accept, endorse, join the system and become one of us, unethical leaders abuse authority.

Diagram 4: Relationship between our actions, our intentions and our impact

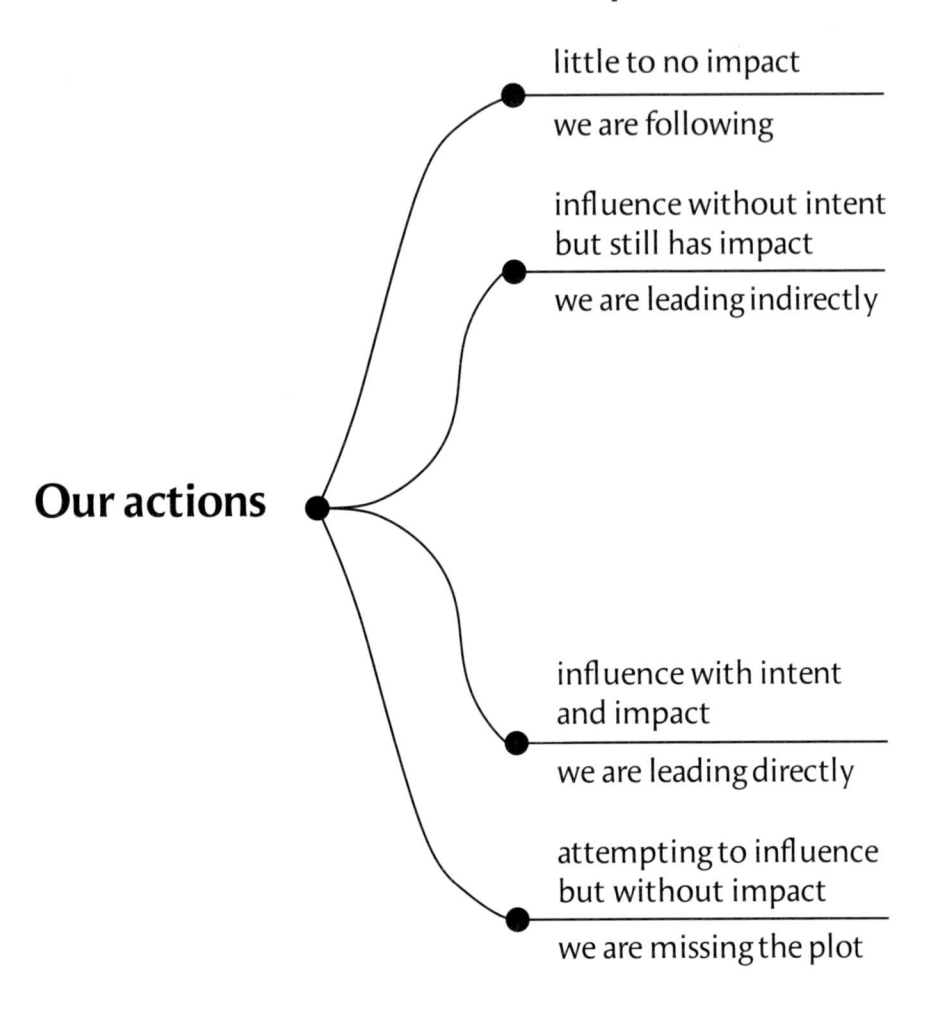

Our actions

- little to no impact
  we are following

- influence without intent but still has impact
  we are leading indirectly

- influence with intent and impact
  we are leading directly

- attempting to influence but without impact
  we are missing the plot

"Purchase the bottled Holy water to secure immediate salvation, send children into crowded areas with explosive devices, kill the Whites, kill the Blacks, kill the Palestinians, kill the Jews, engage in human trafficking, deny women an education, storm the Capital and rape the nation," are unhinged means to achieve unscrupulous ends. Power-loaded, ruthless leaders are hard to stop.

The nature of influence including who can influence whom has changed dramatically over the past 15 years. Scammers and fraudsters have been quick to exploit the vulnerabilities of technologies and end-users to achieve their devious goals. Near universal access to a networked world has created exponential opportunities to influence vast numbers of people across the globe.

Fast-forward to the New Millennium and enter the world of social media, Smartphones and the pervasiveness of the internet. Your world. My world. Everybody's world.

As of April 2023, it was reported that there were 5.18 billion internet users worldwide. This is an estimated 65% of the global population. Social media platforms such as X, formerly Twitter, Meta, formerly Facebook, Instagram, Threads, ShareChat, Roposo, TikTok/Douyin, Koo, WeChat, Sina Weibo and Bilbil share an estimated 4.8 billion users or 60% of the world's population.

That's a lot of ears for a lot of influencers who no longer need credibility to post their opinions. Not facts but opinions extrapolated into universal truths. Any self-appointed social leader suddenly has access to audiences of millions. Virtual badges of honour and plenty of advertising money are now awarded to people who can boast the highest numbers of 'followers'.

Platform owners measure their success by the level of engagement the social leaders can induce from their followers. Decoded that means end-users are expected to: 'Act on their recommendations and directives.' That is action with serious intent to influence.

Diagram 5: Multiple ways in which our actions influence organisations and people

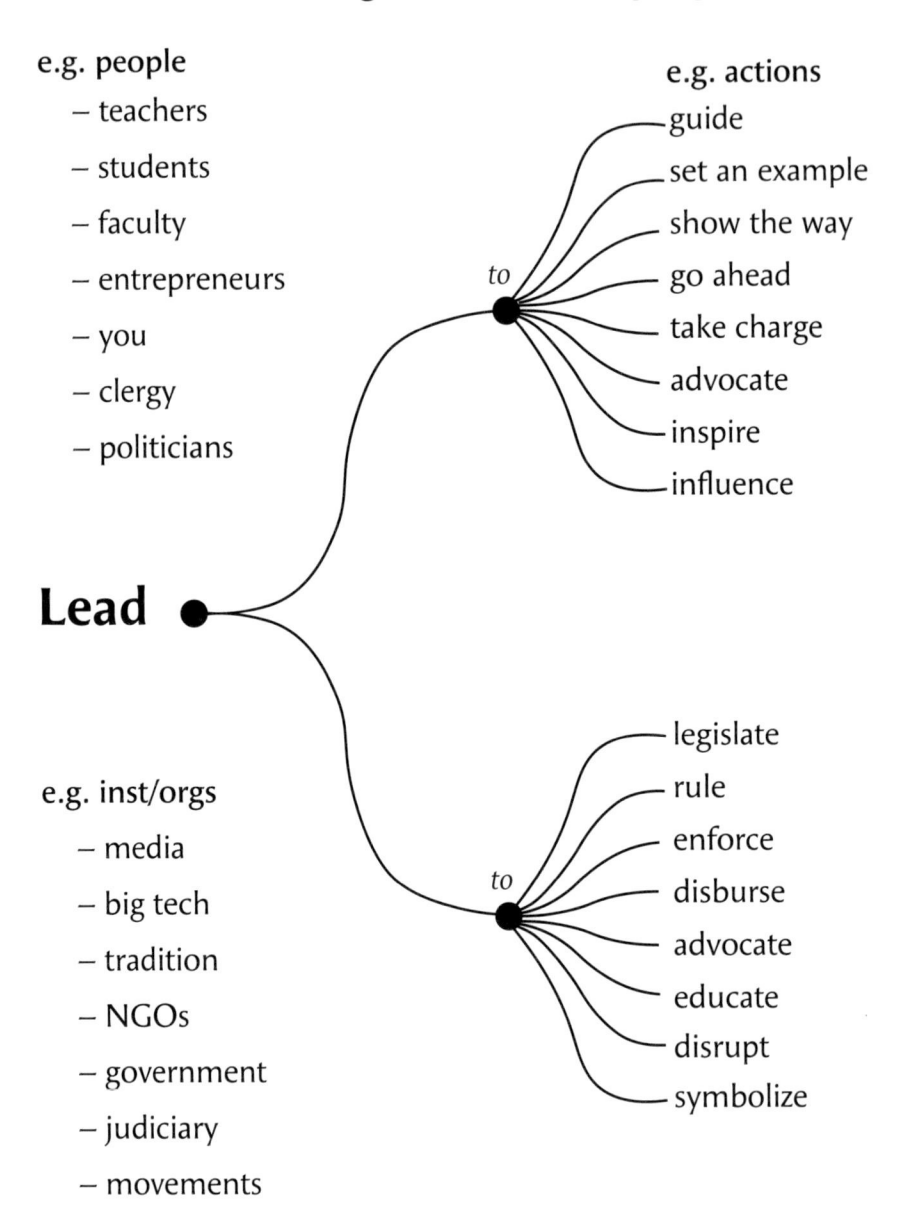

e.g. people
- teachers
- students
- faculty
- entrepreneurs
- you
- clergy
- politicians

e.g. actions
- guide
- set an example
- show the way
- go ahead
- take charge
- advocate
- inspire
- influence

Lead to

e.g. inst/orgs
- media
- big tech
- tradition
- NGOs
- government
- judiciary
- movements

to
- legislate
- rule
- enforce
- disburse
- advocate
- educate
- disrupt
- symbolize

Diagram 6: The crazy world of the internet

**INTERNET OF THINGS –
EVERYTHING CONNECTED TO EVERYTHING**

A Checklist for Leading and Leadership

IN SUMMARY: POINTS TO PONDER

1.
To lead and the process of leading are key enablers of human development dating back 2.6 million years.

2.
Total dependence at birth forces us to follow.

3.
Transitioning from dependence to independence is natural, but not automatic.

4.
That transition requires accepting higher personal ownership and freedom of choice as counter-balances to followership.

5.
Learning to lead and adjusting to life are interrelated, ongoing processes.

6.
Tragically, a significant number of people miss these developmental steps completely.

7.
The influence we have can be intentional and/or consequential.

8.
The capacity to lead can be hijacked for unsavoury purposes.

9.
The most important end – bar none – is how a capacity to lead provides the means to discover and enjoy our potential.

10.
We cannot unsubscribe from leading. We always have influence. The question remains: In what ways?

Leadership Defined

Leadership is the **action(s)** a person takes to achieve **results** through the efforts of **other people**. Leadership is not the art of this or the science of that. Leadership is work, work that requires effort. The work may include many forms of preparation and planning but leadership only comes to life when there is engagement – actions that mobilise other people – to, in turn, take action.

Two things need to be in place for that engagement to occur. Firstly, the leader needs to have some form of authority that will cause people to at least pay attention. Secondly, there needs to be some level of skill although that is frequently not the case. Interestingly, the established practice of searching for the so-called best person for the job often provides the authority for that person to get the attention they need to lead.

Completely dismiss the mythical belief that leaders are born. It's pure nonsense. Of course, all leaders are born – they are people, not gods. But we are not born with the skills that enable us to influence others to take action. Those skills are definable and must be learnt – the earlier the better. More about that later.

The degree of influence a person has, that is, the amount of authority, and the extent of their skills, work in combination along a sliding scale. It's never absolute, seldom permanent and always contextually bound. The battlefields of religious wars, national disputes and ideological purges are soaked with the blood of millions of people who refused to yield to the power of leaders they would not obey.

Context counts. We all live and work in multiple contexts – some close and immediate, others distant and delayed. They are constantly evolving and changing even for people and communities who would prefer it not to be so. The manner in which leaders choose to engage, which is referred to as their style, must take account of the contextual variables and should be adjusted accordingly.

The nature of the actions for which the leader is mobilising support, the people involved, the available time, the risk and the complexity are minimum considerations. Legislation, lead times to implementation and desired completion, cultural nuances, resource requirements and competitor responses are a few of the larger contextual variables that senior leaders in business will need to consider.

Leaders in politics and government will have their own set of unique contextual variables. Entrepreneurs and venture capitalists know full well that the timing of innovations must be in sync with market opportunities and their context. No matter how promising an innovation is, too early or too late to market can be a kiss of death.

Leaders in education who allow themselves to become outdated and out of touch with reality, are unlikely to proactively provide the leadership that will keep curricula relevant and appealing. Contexts matter a great deal, and they are becoming increasingly messy, harder to define and volatile. Ask any parent.

Retaining contextual relevance is both important and challenging in a dynamically changing world. How this can be achieved is addressed later in the section dealing with the primary roles of leaders.

Skills count, and they are, in the age where knowledge has become power, the most important foundation for effective leadership. Wealth and status have their limitations. **There are no magical secrets to leadership**. Claims and revelations of that sort should be seen for what they are – snake oil to be avoided.

The real power of leadership skills is compounded when they form part of the other underlying capabilities in your basket of competences – personal and functional/technical. You'll find an exciting section on competences, and how they can be developed, just up ahead.

Securing that understanding and acceptance – simply abbreviated as 'U/A' – is the golden knot leaders must get tied to be effective. Emailing instructions, distributing notices, launching appeals on social media and boycotting a class are examples of popular actions that call for action of some sort. They are incomplete and frankly a failure from a leadership perspective, where they fail to secure declared acceptance. This requires imbedding through ongoing repetition and checking.

> *u/a: no understand, no can do; no accept, no will do.*
> *u/a: no understand, no can do; no accept, no will do.*
> *u/a: no understand, no can do; no accept, no will do.*
> *u/a: no understand, no can do; no accept, no will do.*

For many years, a colleague shared her aspiration of visiting the great lakes of Canada, travelling to see the bears feast on the salmon swimming upstream to their traditional spawning grounds, and simply, indulging in the great natural beauty of the country. Without exception, her friends agreed – it was an appealing idea. When she invited them to take a break from their daily routines and get a loan to fund the trip, no one accepted.

People may agree with the actions leaders wish to take, but if they don't accept them and/or the leader, the desired results will not be forthcoming. Mobilising people to achieve results requires understanding and acceptance. Period.

Diagram 7: Expanded Definition of Leadership

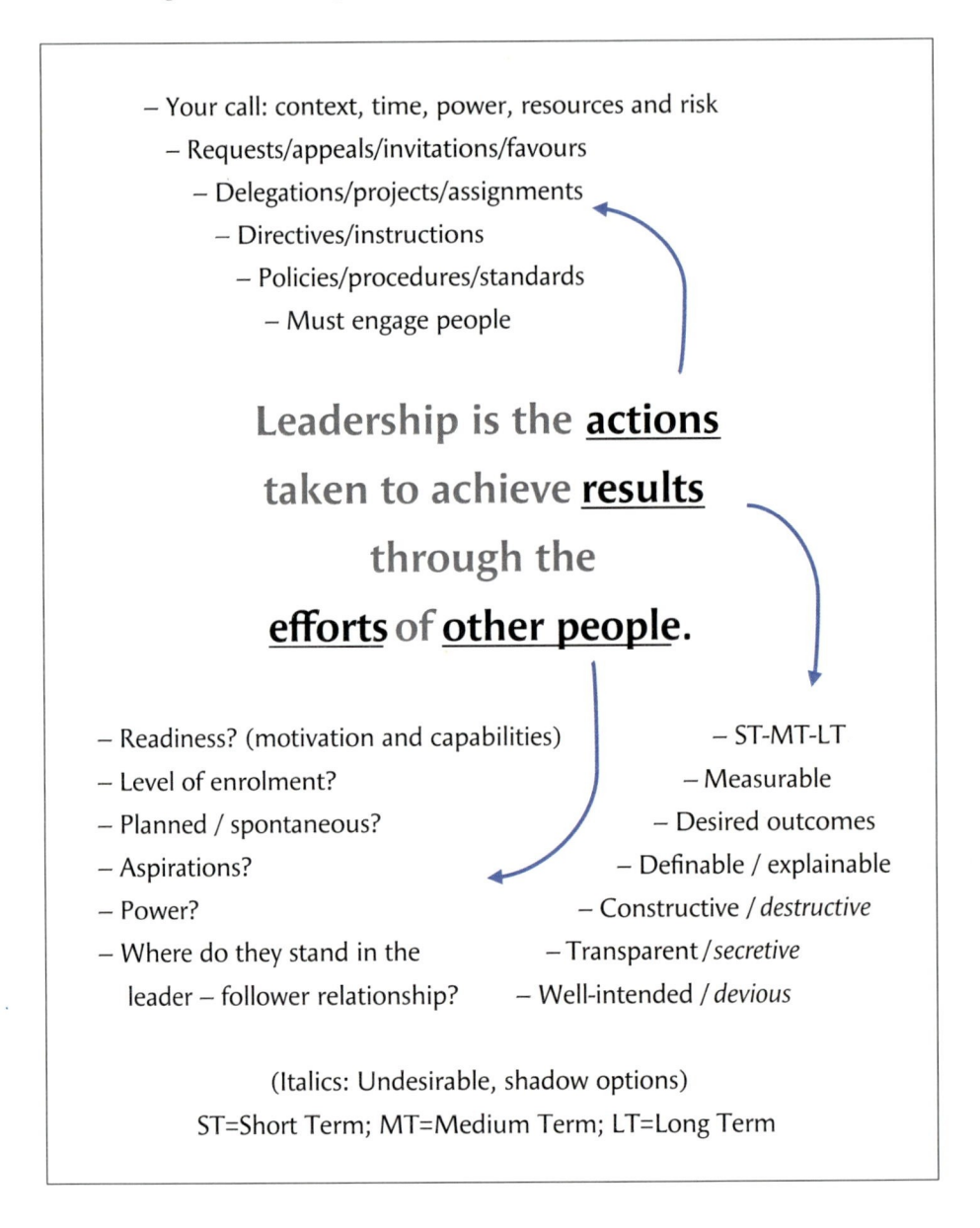

– Your call: context, time, power, resources and risk
  – Requests/appeals/invitations/favours
    – Delegations/projects/assignments
      – Directives/instructions
        – Policies/procedures/standards
          – Must engage people

Leadership is the **actions** taken to achieve **results** through the **efforts** of **other people**.

– Readiness? (motivation and capabilities)   – ST-MT-LT
– Level of enrolment?   – Measurable
– Planned / spontaneous?   – Desired outcomes
– Aspirations?   – Definable / explainable
– Power?   – Constructive / *destructive*
– Where do they stand in the   – Transparent / *secretive*
   leader – follower relationship?   – Well-intended / *devious*

(Italics: Undesirable, shadow options)
ST=Short Term; MT=Medium Term; LT=Long Term

Taking it from a slightly different angle:
- Leadership entails 'intentional' actions to 'influence' (mobilise) others to pursue goals, adopt ideas, align with

ideologies, complete tasks and act in ways they probably would not have, without leadership intervention.

- High-impact leaders 'proactively adjust' their leadership style and approach based on the 'people' involved, the desired 'results' and 'situational variables' such as time, complexity, risk and return. Flexibility and relevance is the name of the game.

- Leading occurs 24/7. Leadership is 'task, people and context' specific.

- Leadership is 'not limited to formal roles' and mandates. Parents provide leadership without formal mandates.

- 'Positions and titles' are not needed to lead, and they don't certify the holder as a person who can.

- Leadership is a 'means to many ends' not an end in itself. As the late Stephen Covey wisely wrote in *The 7 Habits of Highly Successful People*, 'start with the end in mind'.

- Unless you are in the armed or security forces, and even then, there are exceptions, 'compliance' with leadership directives is 'never automatically compulsory'.

- How that works requires an understanding of the 'power' that comes with 'authority'.

- No matter what, people have the 'right to accept or reject'. Leaders cannot force people to act where they choose not to, even where the consequence may lead to their demise or even death – such as occurs in totalitarian regimes.

- People who 'disrespect this right' and seek to lead by invoking subservience to nations, themselves or causes, are 'not leaders', but 'slave masters and manipulators'.

- People who 'lead, also follow'. The reverse is not automatically true.

> As the artist mixes colours and textures to create new beauty, the leader mixes life to craft new meanings and purpose.

Influence that comes with Positional Authority

If we can't get the engine to start, having a car is of little value as a means of transport. Having great ideas that involve other people, may be commendable. They are wasted unless you can get them adopted and acted upon. In leadership terms, that requires influence – the engine – that gets the car moving. No influence, no leadership.

There are two main **sources of influence**:

- Authority that has the power to enforce action and compliance – positional authority.

- Authority that induces action based on the relationship between the leader and those he/she seeks to mobilise – personal authority.

Both are important.

Positional authority is influence linked to positions and titles that are formally defined, and legitimately recognised. Persons who legitimately occupy such positions have the right to apply authority over people who are subject to the prescriptions the authority provides.

Employment in all sectors of the economy includes some form of hierarchical arrangement with authority linked to positions. In schools, colleges and universities, teaching staff have varying degrees of positional authority over students whether the latter like it or not. The same applies from small mom-and-pop family businesses to NGOs and even criminal cartels.

Netflix, Patagonia, Nordstrom, FedEx and Bridgewater are iconic examples of large organisations that have completely re-scripted how positional power can be shared with staff through ownership and self-control. The default mode of top-down control is not the only way in which positional power can be effectively harnessed.

There are hundreds of smaller organisations from literally every sector in economies worldwide that are rewriting the rules relating to influence with positional authority. The dominant trend is the devolution of power – spreading it far and wide – in workforces to:

- Improve the speed of decision-making.
- Improve the quality and contextualisation of decision-making.
- Nurture staff ownership and innovation.
- Build work cultures where people can genuinely experience greater meaning and fulfilment.

Fast Company Magazine publishes an annual list, normally in the first quarter of the year, listing the companies they regard as the 'most innovative'. A consistent feature of those companies is the manner in which they share positional power.

The value and importance of well-defined positional authority can also be found in organisations such as Greenpeace (International), a multi-national voluntary organisation working in the environmental area, BRAC, one of the world's largest non-governmental development organisations working to alleviate poverty and empower women in Bangladesh, and SEWA, the Self-Employed Women's Association in India. They are well structured and dependent on the discipline that flows from positional authority.

The authority vested in the holder of a position ends when they no longer hold the position. The authority is linked to the position, not the person.

Positional authority does not extend to an incumbent's family, and friends although many do try to secure leverage by mentioning a connection, past or current. "Allow me to introduce myself. I'm the owner's son, and I need a favour."

Position and authority are not synonymous or automatic. Many positions such as honorary secretary or volunteer para-medic have no vested authority. Although they carry considerable responsibility, even parents have limited positional authority.

The extent and limits of positional authority should always be clarified by and for the people affected by the authority. An absence of this clarity is a common source of frustration and abuse. Ask any person who has accepted a position with supposed authority only to later discover they have little to no authority at all. Marriages that subjugate women to an existence without any say or authority are a similar evil.

The #MeToo movement revealed how powerful men in business, media and the entertainment industries, used positional authority to leverage sexual favours without shame or conscience. Intelligence agencies and military organisations are known to abuse the rights and powers vested in them under the guise of national security.

The key takeaways here are:

- The holders of formal leadership positions should always clarify – ideally in writing – the extent and boundaries of any rights and powers linked to the positions.

- Rights and powers beyond those defined, can be expanded subject to the merits of the situation coupled with transparency and accountability.

- **High-achieving individuals** recognise the importance of positional authority when mobilising people to achieve results. Although they will not hesitate to use that authority should it be required, their preference is to rather nurture and use personal authority.

- Never abuse positional authority and never allow yourself to become a victim of such abuse. Your leading matters.

Influence that comes with Personal Authority

We all have personal authority. What is it and where does it come from? Talented people with enviable track records of success, and excellent credentials are inclined to think they are the source of the authority.

People should defer to them. Wrong.

People in formal leadership positions frequently make the same mistake. Apart from the positional authority they hold, they assume that personal credentials such as qualifications, experience, seniority, and track records of success, literally anything that creates positive impressions, will cause people to be receptive to their personal influence. Those are useful starting points but the assumption is again wrong.

We are not the source of our personal power. The source is other people who are prepared to accept our leadership based on their perceptions of our credibility. Their acceptance is the key ingredient. The perceptions may be objective and grounded in facts. They may be subjective, and loaded with positive and/or negative biases. Irrespective, they make the judgement call whether they follow or not.

"You will listen to me! I am your father!" Why?

Does the title father or mother imply submission? It did for centuries, and it still does for kids up to their early teens. Youngsters have come to learn that respecting their parents does not include mandatory submission. The same template applies in a broader society where titles such as 'manager', 'supervisor', 'boss', 'professor', 'senior' and 'rabbi' have no embedded authority.

We no longer trust titles. That age has passed. We want and deserve more than just a title when opening ourselves up to the influence of others. They too deserve no less from us. Despite considerable research on the subject, there is still no consensus on which factors provide better indicators of a person's credibility titles. They are merely starting points, useful references.

The limitations of aggregating value judgements into universal truths can be misleading. They lose the unique qualities that earn awesome, frequently global, personal authority. Richard Branson of Virgin Atlantic, Nelson Mandela, Gandhi, Liz Cheney, Angela Merkel, Oprah Winfrey and Amina J Mohamed (United Nations Deputy Secretary-General) are a few of the many outliers who defy the norms of convention.

Even strangers can influence strangers by their mere presence or absence. Watch how people change the route they are walking when they observe an innocent, yet dangerous-looking person on a park bench just ahead of them. There is no connection between the parties, but the park bencher has, probably with no intention at all, influenced the path being walked.

Perhaps the personal influence in our example would be different if it occurred on a crowded street with two police officers walking ahead – a different context. Perhaps the park bencher would be ignored if the people were armed – a different perception about the other person – not seen as a threat. Culture and context again count. Declaring ourselves credible does not make us credible no matter how valid our contention may be. We have to earn the right to be heard not simply claim the right on terms of our choosing. That requires being 'others focussed' to understand what it is they value and respect. The best way to achieve that is via direct interaction and relationship building.

Leaders who recognise the pivotal importance of making those connections use a variety of approaches to facilitate interaction. This includes personally meeting new team members, scholars, students – whoever is joining a group – setting up one-on-one meetings, arranging small functions, joint training, Town Hall Meetings and involvement at every opportunity. Internet conferencing is undoubtedly a poor second prize, but it beats doing nothing.

The weekly store visits, and ongoing interactions with suppliers undertaken by Walmart's founder, the late Sam Walton, were legendary. Who will ever forget the visits that did or did not take place to your schoolroom by a former headmaster?

Influence based on perceived credibility can emerge without the affected parties having met or even knowing about each other's existence. I have never met Daniel Kahneman, Nobel Laureate in Behavioural Economics, Richard Feynman, Nobel Laureate in Physics, David Whyte and Professor Leo Buscaglia.

Their work and approach to life have influenced me profoundly. I regard them as highly credible and worth following. Their personal authority – influence in my context – is significant. You may feel entirely different. That's the beauty of personal authority – other people, not you – get to decide how receptive they will be to your work, what you stand for, and your believability.

Unlike positional authority which is hierarchical and top-down in nature, personal authority is 4-way multi-directional. In hierarchical structures, positional authority only applies downwards – power over people. By contrast, personal authority can be earned with peers, with seniors and juniors within any structures in which you operate, and most significantly of all, with any individuals – near and far, known and unknown, outside those structures.

We should all think deeply and clearly about the factors we value in determining credibility. Our conclusions will assist with the development of our own credibility. More importantly, we will hopefully have credible reasons for being open and receptive – or not – to the influence of others. Without a filter of that nature, we are at risk of being vulnerable to our own naivety.

Try something new. Consider the factors you regard as important for credibility and trust. Mine are set out in Diagram 8. There is no requirement for consensus.

When the Thomas Webb Telescope was under construction, the project team identified 344 'single-point failures' – events which should they occur, could singularly derail the project in its entirety.

Honesty and reliability are potential single-point failures. Do you trust a person you know is dishonest? Would people trust you? What's the value of competence and resourcefulness when we cannot rely on a person to pitch up? Gaps in competence and other foundations can be addressed. Correcting breakdowns in honesty and reliability are hard to repair. Our word is our bond and a commitment made is a commitment kept.

There is no such thing as being half pregnant, mostly honest and reasonably reliable. Pursuing that route leaves you being half-trustworthy. We are or we are not.

Diagram 8: Primary foundations of credibility

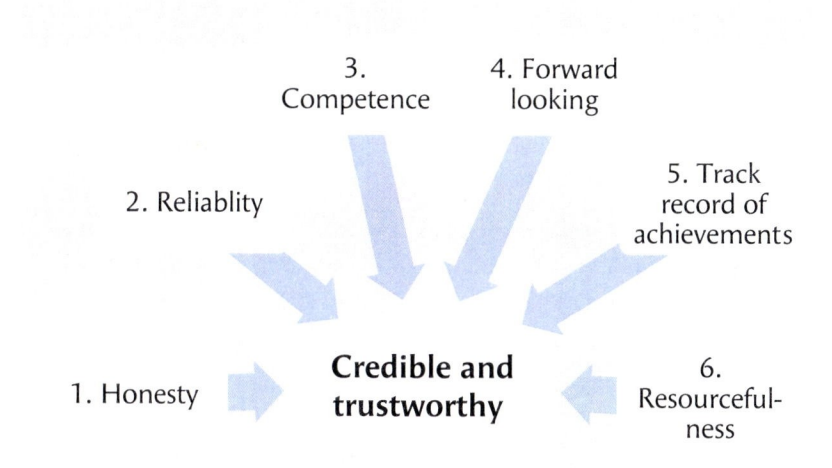

1. Honesty
2. Reliablity
3. Competence
4. Forward looking
5. Track record of achievements
6. Resourcefulness

→ **Credible and trustworthy**

Summary: Positional and personal authority

	Positional	Personal
What it is	Rights and powers to make decisions and expect compliance based on legitimate mandates/delegations	Attention and cooperation given to us based on perceptions of our credibility and trustworthiness
Source	Legitimate rights and powers linked to legitimate positions which the legitimate incumbent is authorised to apply	Other people
Nature	Authority over the work, work routines, performance standards and deployment for which people have been contracted and have an obligation to fulfil	Authority based on shared understanding and ongoing contracting – an influence that stems from the perceptions other people have

A Checklist for Leading and Leadership

	Positional	Personal
Span of authority	Authority 'over' people within the jurisdiction of the 'leader', typically 'downwards' within specific boundaries in an organisational setting, laterally and upwards only by exceptional determinations	Contextually bound authority with people across any boundaries and in any direction – colleagues, seniors, family, friends, strangers, proteges, students and literally any constituency
Timeframe	The incumbent holds the authority as long as they hold the position	For the period, you are regarded as credible and trustworthy
Delegation	Positional authority and related responsibilities can be delegated unless there are prescribed embargoes.	Does not apply.

Other Influencers: Seduction, Fear, Manipulation and Intimidation

Influence derived from positional and personal authority, when correctly used, is transparent, open and legitimate. Unfortunately, there are other methods of influence such as seduction, invoking fear, manipulation and the use of intimidation to induce and mobilise people to action.

Extortion, blackmail, torture, indoctrination and false promises are some of the methods used by 'influencers' to induce the responses they want from unwilling people. The argument used, especially by clandestine operatives in intelligence agencies and authoritarian politicians, is the classical 'ends justify means' narrative.

The supposed evil threats posed by some designated target – individual or entire populations, as unilaterally decided by the enforcer, are used to justify any methods, no matter how cruel or inhumane, to extract the desired responses. Gullible voters are regularly manipulated using conspiracy theories, calls to the past and the repeated use of outright lies.

The Gold Standard of Trust

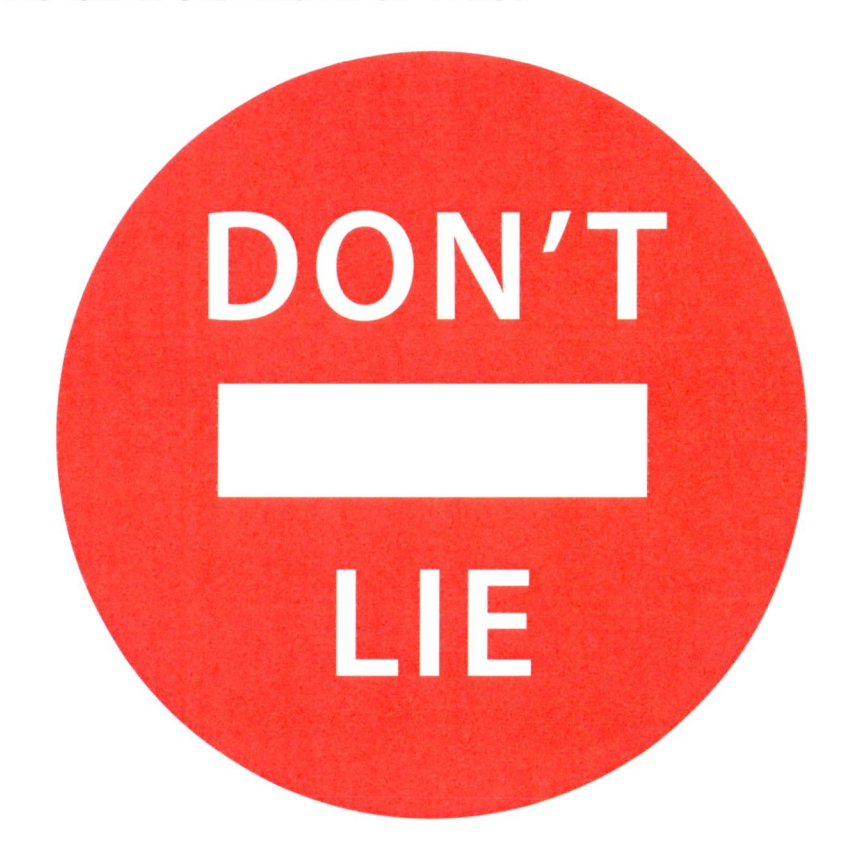

DON'T LIE

IF YOU EVER WANT TO COUNT FOR SOMETHING IN LIFE, DON'T LIE AND DON'T LIE ABOUT LIES.

The meeting is a waste of time. We smile. The rabbi talks nonsense. We smile. The relationship is destructive. We avoid dealing with it. We are treated with disrespect. We are hurt. We pretend it is not so. We allow it to avoid possible rejection or conflict. They are lies.

We have inbuilt auto routines that insulate us from our lies. 'I never lie' is one of them – as though that thinking error – because you believe it, makes it real. "I'm a good person who does not want to hurt you – that's why I avoid telling you what I truly think. You cannot handle the truth." The 'not want to hurt you' provides the first convenient justification for the lie, and the 'you can't handle it' provides the second. Have you ever wondered how much more hurt you would be if you knew people – especially significant others – lied to you?

The Gold Standard for trust is to not lie. Any person achieving the standard will be well ahead of the majority of any population. People can look each other in the eye and tell the exact opposite of what they are truly thinking, in a manner that is undetectable. You can. I can.

Others can. Am I right or wrong? Don't lie.

Chris Argyris, a former Yale and Harvard Professor described lies as cover-ups – attempts to bypass the truth. His research revealed that people can, with considerable skill, not only cover up the truth but also add several more layers of cover-ups. People lie; it gets challenged; they deny the lie; the denial gets challenged; they deny the denial.

> Person A: "All the talk about fossil fuels and their related emissions causing climate change is just a hoax."
>
> Person B: "That's not true. That's a lie."
>
> Person A: "Look, let me show you the latest statistics released by the Coal Producers Association."

Person B: "You're using selective, biased data to mislead me."

Person A: "Would I ever lie to you?" Where does this masterful skill originate?

You may be surprised, but our parents, and centuries of flawed cultural practices have taught us how to skilfully lie. We learn so well we get to a point where we cannot even detect it in our behaviour. Should you be a parent, the chances are pretty good you have taught your kids how to lie with both ease and justification, as though the latter makes it acceptable.

Watch young children. They describe the world exactly as they see it, without any pretence. If they dislike something about you, that's what they'll call it. A parent overhearing the child's statement, takes them aside for a gentle reprimand: "You cannot say that to your Grandmother."

"But, Mum, she does look old."

"Maybe, but you cannot say that because you will embarrass her. You could even cause some conflict. Worse still, your Grandmother may reject you." Without the cognitive development to recognise how openness and honesty are being hard-wired as wrong when the possibility of embarrassment, conflict or rejection exists, the youngster is programmed for life.

There are numerous larger-than-life examples of public figures being caught lying. Former President Bill Clinton addressed the American nation regarding his relationship with Monica Lewinsky on 26 January 1998. In a televised speech, broadcast to the world, Clinton stated, "I did not have sexual relations with that woman, Miss Lewinsky." His statement was a lie.

A former prime minister of Britain, Boris Johnson, was stripped of his Parliamentary privileges by his peers in 2023 after lying about social functions that violated COVID restrictions. A senior Volkswagen executive was sentenced to seven years in prison in

2017 after he and six other executives including the Chairman, were indicted for concealing software used to evade USA pollution limits on nearly 600,000 diesel vehicles.

In January 2021, the *Washington Post* reported the staggering 30,573 false or misleading claims made by former President Trump while in office. **Lying does not belong in leading**. Whatever happened to "thou shalt not lie or bare false witness?"

Trust is the foundation and glue for lasting relationships. It goes hand in hand with respect, brings people closer and is a catalyst for high-impact leadership.

If you apply only one lesson from this book, it should be this: ***"Get back in touch with what integrity really means."*** No half measures. No so-called white lies, and rationalisations to justify lies.

Lying is a destructive self-defeating habit. Breaking it requires unlearning the deeply programmed routines used to avoid rejection, conflict and embarrassment. Those outcomes are normal parts of life. They are not evils to be avoided at all costs. They are behaviours frequently observed in submissive, passive individuals.

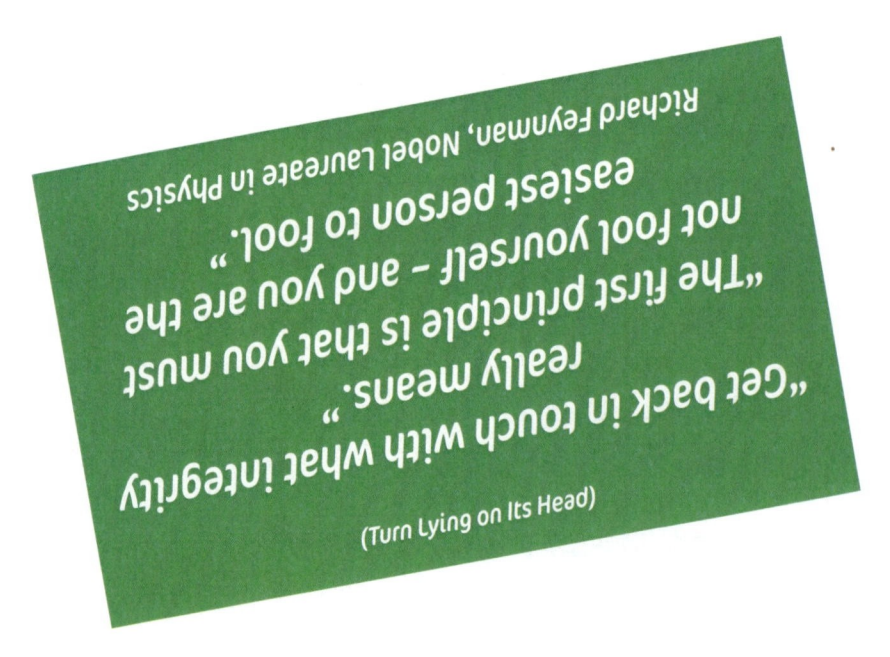

"The first principle is that you must not fool yourself – and you are the easiest person to fool."
Richard Feynman, Nobel Laureate in physics

"Get back in touch with what integrity really means."

(Turn Lying on Its Head)

IN SUMMARY: POINTS TO PONDER

1.
Leading and leadership are related but not the same.

2.
Two metrics for effective leadership stand out above the rest. Is it relevant? Does it have impact?

3.
All the other descriptors for leaders and leadership such as good, great, hero, game-changer, spiritual, others-centric and so on, are simply poster material for movies.

4.
To lead is to influence.

5.
To influence with intent, we require authority (power).

6.
The two primary sources of authority (power) are positional and personal.

7.
We should be clear on who has what power to avoid abuse and over-reach.

8.
No authority should ever be absolute and above question.

9.
It takes a lifetime to build and maintain the credibility that enables personal authority. It takes seconds of indiscretion and poor judgment to destroy it.

10.
Reliability, honesty, and competence are the minimum requirements for authentic, credible authority.

The Role of Competence in Leadership

Competence is another one of those everyday concepts that is taken for granted without being fully understood. Most if not all professional, and technical professions have defined standards which people must meet in order to practice the profession. There are controlling associations, testing authorities, and even legislation which regulates standards, and certification.

Mariners, teachers, lawyers, accountants, scientists, aviators, engineers, technologists, and musicians are examples from hundreds of domains that specify minimum standards of competence. The domain of leadership has none.

Honesty and reliability are the chips that allow us to sit at the credibility table. Competences provide the means we need to participate. Competences are central to success in life, and a prerequisite for people who want to make the most of their potential. Competences unlock and create potential, and from a leadership point of view, equip us to support others to do the same.

Select any role that involves some form of intentional leadership – achieving results through the efforts of other people – and you will find a need to coach, train, guide, encourage and support the people involved. Leaders are both activists and catalysts for personal growth and performance improvement.

This may seem obvious. Surprisingly though, I've lost count of the endless debates with knowledgeable, accomplished individuals, who, believe it or not, just don't get 'the competence thing'.

If you would like to see eyes roll over with long pauses of silence, ask people: "To what do you attribute your success?" Be assured that it will be an insightful experience. Try answering the question yourself. "To what do you attribute your success?"

Responses that omit some reference to competences fall well short of accuracy. We can bend it whichever way we want.

Competences, track record of delivery, support from others along the way and luck are the primary enablers of success.

Competence is a specific capacity an individual holds that enables them to successfully complete tasks to a standard and to conduct themselves effectively. A competence comprises a collection of underlying parts that causally, not randomly or accidentally, provide the means to successfully complete the task(s) and deployment.

Diagram 9: Generic underlying parts of a competence

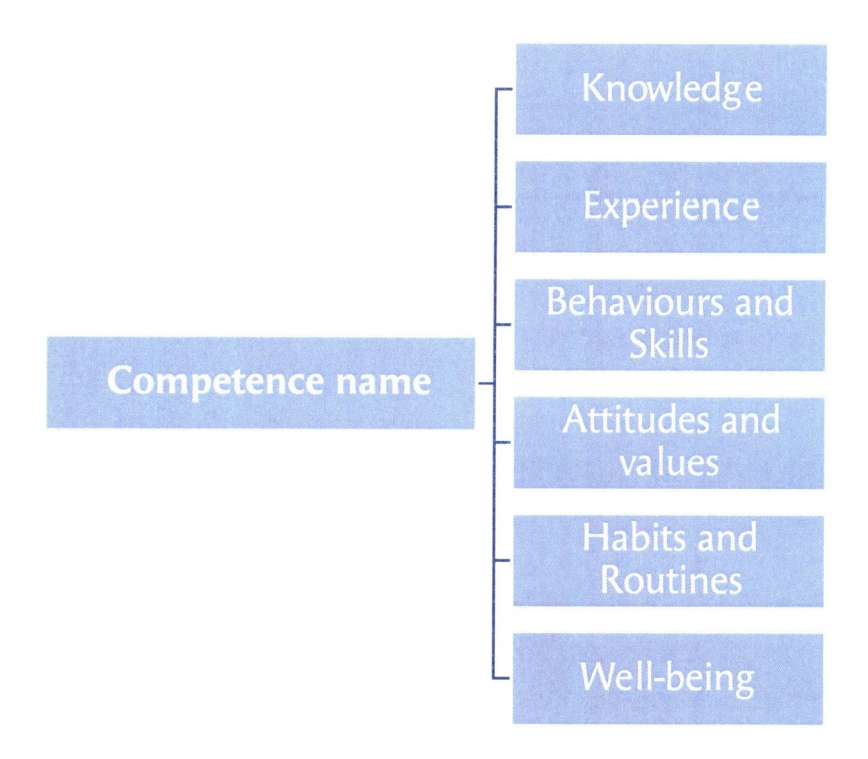

```
                              ┌── Knowledge
                              │
                              ├── Experience
                              │
                              ├── Behaviours and Skills
Competence name ──────────────┤
                              ├── Attitudes and values
                              │
                              ├── Habits and Routines
                              │
                              └── Well-being
```

The optimum mix and relative importance will vary depending on the nature of the task and deployment standards. For example, the underlying parts for competence in advanced computational mathematics versus deep sea trawling versus marketing and sales will differ dramatically yet could also partially overlap.

A Checklist for Leading and Leadership

The underlying parts work together like the parts in a system. All are needed in the right proportions for the system to work. All the parts influence each other and the effectiveness of the system – in this case, uniquely for each person, depends on how well the parts work together.

An understanding of the parts of competence enables us to focus on very specific areas of development. Assume you want to improve your capacity to lead. Must you work on your knowledge of leadership models and/or improve your problem-solving skills and/or nurture your psychological robustness? That level of pragmatic detail makes an enormous difference for us personally and those whose development we support. Experienced coaches do not advise their players to simply improve their game. They drill down into all the relevant parts of the competence required for specific levels of performance. Coaching is an integral part of what we do both formally and informally as leaders.

Age, new technologies, shifts in strategies, circumstances and job priorities, can all trigger the need to adjust aspects of competence and even the mix of the collection or basket of competences a person holds. Future-focussed leaders and individuals try to anticipate these shifts so that they can initiate unlearning and relearning in advance of the shifts.

For example, consider how computing skills have become mainstream and the challenge that presents to individuals who trained during an analogue age. Airline pilots who have to re-skill to 'fly by wire' in 'glass cockpits.' Ask people who made the tough transition in middle age from being a successful parent to being a struggling beginner grandparent. What about the considerable competence gap that must be filled when individuals are promoted from being technical/functional specialists to supervisory roles. Educators who become departmental heads; Cabbies who become despatchers; Lawyers and accountants who become directors/partners; The list is never ending as are the requirements for ongoing competence adjustments – adding, refining and discarding.

Competence development flows from being a beginner (novice) to a norm performer (meeting the standards of an average performer in a role). Individuals who are not content with the crowded pool of average, continue along the development path to superior and even masterful.

The difference between these four levels is visible in the behaviours associated with them.

- **Beginner:** Hesitant, lacking confidence, absence of fluency, discrete actions, unforced error with supervision being required;

- **Norm:** Fluent, confident, holistic completion of tasks, minimum error and supervision;

- **Superior:** High fluency and efficiency, seamless in deployment and task completion with holistic integration of knowledge, skills, routines and error by extreme exception;

- **Masterful:** Thought leader recognised by peers as a role model for innovation and achievement within a credible context.

Higher competence as a collective of the parts not just simply one or two aspects, equips us to deal with greater complexity. Having a brain filled with more knowledge is compromised where the skills and emotional maturity to apply have been neglected.

I want to stress **holistic**. There are zillions of examples of highly recommended routines, positive attitudes and essential skills. None should be adopted blindly and without considering how they fit – work together with the other parts. And just as important, their suitability for you.

In a widely acclaimed Commencement Speech, Admiral William McRaven shared a list of ten routines that US Navy Seals use as a code of conduct. One of them focusses on the importance of being able to endure many forms of hardship – physical, emotional and so on, and the reassurance such experience provides, to not easily give up, or as the Seals describe it, to not 'Ring the Bell'.

That is a valuable – perhaps even life-saving routine if you are a Navy Seal. It could be a counter-productive routine if you are in a career that offers no intrinsic satisfaction. Knowing when and how to quit a toxic relationship or soul-destroying activity requires just as much emotional courage as enduring physical pain. Rejection, failure, doubt and loneliness are common features of life, especially for people who lead. People who lack psychological robustness and personal pride, find themselves on emotional roller coasters. The fortitude to not easily 'Ring the Bell', is not a matter of good luck. High standards of competence that have been carefully cultivated, provide more luck than you can imagine. What we include or exclude in our competence framework (portfolio/basket of competences) matters a great deal.

Diagram 10 illustrates how the experience of a 'beginner' is repeated at every level of competence development. It is helpful to recognise the 'stepping stone' effect in the process of competence development. It is not a simple linear progression from beginner to mastery. Moving from one level to another entails starting as a beginner for that level (hesitant, lacking fluency and confidence).

Working through these transitions takes considerable maturity and patience. It requires plenty of repetition and practice to internalise new levels of competence.

The implications of those transitions are seldom welcomed by professionals and individuals who see themselves on a career fast track. Successful people don't easily relate to the notion that as they progress in life, there are many occasions when they are in effect, still beginners.

Diagram 10: Stepping stone effect of progressive development

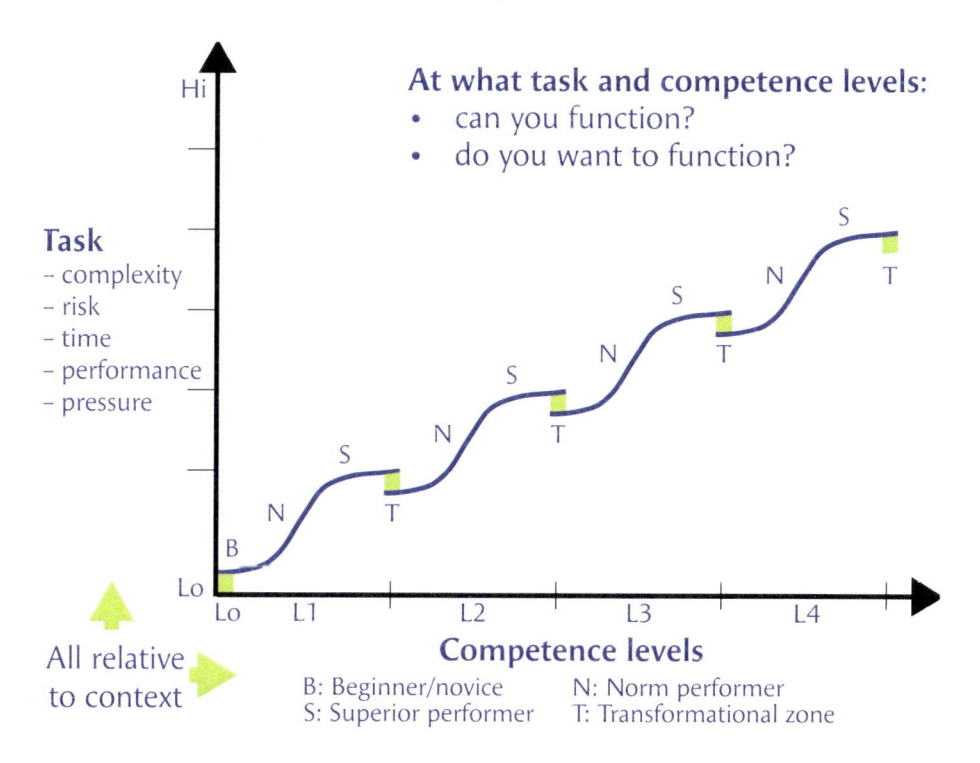

At what task and competence levels:
- can you function?
- do you want to function?

Task
- complexity
- risk
- time
- performance
- pressure

All relative to context

Competence levels
B: Beginner/novice
S: Superior performer
N: Norm performer
T: Transformational zone

Diagram 11 in turn illustrates how changing complexity which goes with personal growth and career advancement, depends on continued competence development. In her blockbuster publication, *Mindsets*, Carol Dweck refers to people with open and adaptive minds versus those who are closed to new possibilities.

We can add, whether by conscious intent or years of experience, a little something to the way we do things. Those additions customise our competences further and provide unique expressions of self. That allows us to move beyond aggregated templates of competences with homogenised ways of thinking, behaving and delivering. These small additions are frequently barely discernible yet exponentially valuable.

A Checklist for Leading and Leadership

Diagram 11: Relationship between task standards and competence

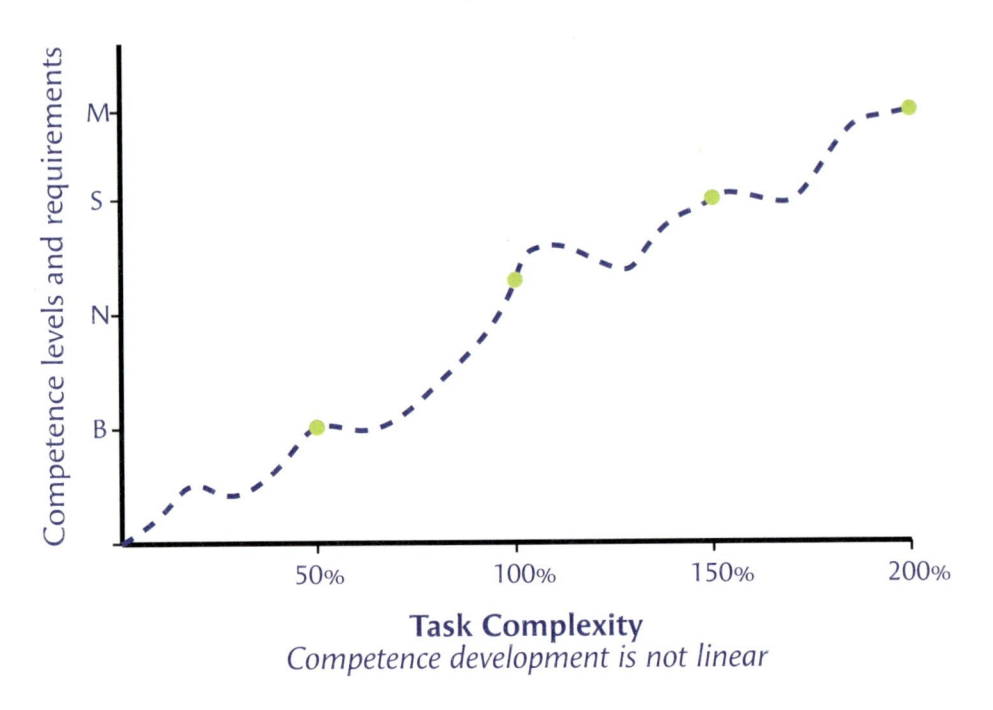

Task Complexity
Competence development is not linear

Here's an example. Behaviour analysis research conducted by Neil Rackham and his Huthwaite Research Group, revealed that negotiators who have the best track record of 'successful implementations' of negotiated deals – by far the most important metric, will openly:

- Draw the other party's attention to any point they think may have been misunderstood – especially if it's to the other party's detriment.

- Allow for a re-negotiation of the point, and,

- Will not intentionally try to mislead or manipulate the other party.

This is frankly counter-intuitive high competence.

These are counter-intuitive actions which at first glance may seem to compromise a negotiation. They follow this approach because they apply a very different metric for the success of a negotiation. Their concern is the **successful implementation** of what is agreed and not merely that an agreement has been reached.

This is superior performance that flows from superior competence and especially barely discernible differences. The top coaches and high-achieving sports teams know the value of finding and focussing on these differences to build world-class performance. For example, they use notational analysis to track speed, passing accuracy, consistency, rate, and types of errors. They search deeply for differentiating details.

This applies equally to relationships and our other areas of engagement such as religious practice, community service, parenting and well-being. "What competence will take us to the next level? What possibilities will the next level open? What are the competences, and especially those barely discernible differences, that will enable our future success over the short, medium and long term?" That surely is something to think about on a regular basis.

Did You Play Your Twiddly Bits?

One evening following what he regarded as a frustrating performance, Mark Knopfler, the remarkable guitarist who founded the internationally famous band – Dire Straits – told his wife that "no matter what I did this evening, I just couldn't get into the songs as I normally do."

To this, she asked: "Did you play your Twiddly Bits?"

"Well no I didn't," he replied.

"Well now, there you have the answer to your problem," she quietly pointed out. You can listen to many renditions of 'Sultans of Swing' by an impressive list of highly accomplished guitarists. Many are superb. None come close to the magic Mark Knopfler produces. It's those Twiddly Bits.

What are yours?

There is much that can be learnt about life, leading and competence from music. There are not many things in life more precious than being loved for the value you bring to people. Music does that. Musicians do that. People who lead well do that. Without sharply focussed and highly developed competences, there would be no music, no musicians of note or leaders worth supporting. External standards and circumstances will influence the competences we select to secure employment and remain in touch with our realities. Our selection may not always be what we want or what we can afford. We may face constraints.

Constraints should not prevent us from selecting holistically and keeping in mind that competence – ignoring the possibility of luck – precedes success. Individually and as leaders, we nurture our competences to meet current challenges and to create future opportunities.

Selecting and being deeply immersed in the development of our competences is not a clinical, bolt-on exercise. It lies at the heart of our ownership and desire to make the most of our life. I'll gladly join forces with a leader who shares that view and can make a pragmatic contribution to the journey.

Note: Dire Straits' recording of 'Sultans of Swing' can be heard on the music services listed below, among other places. You may find the lyrics to verses 1 and 6 particularly appropriate.

- www.amazon.co.uk/music/player/albums/B09ZMVPSZM?trackAsin=B09ZMPFG2C

- open.spotify.com/track/
  37Tmv4NnfQeb0ZgUC4fOJj?
  si=b6e871e5959b4ad3

- music.apple.com/us/album/
  sultans-of-swing/307029087?i=307029144

The band can also be seen in action in this famous video:

- www.youtube.com/watch?v=h0ffIJ7ZO4U

Email:

From: Wessel

To: Ian

MY TWIDDLY BITS FOR HOLLANDAISE SAUCE

Work presses heavily still. We did not close by our end of June quarter, but that is not a train smash as we will get it done in the next few days.

Other things can wait, but I cannot let your question about hollandaise dangle too much longer. Sadly, very many things can, and will, ruin a hollandaise. Foremost, cooking the sabayon too quickly will turn it into scrambled eggs. As with all egg things, slow and low is better than quick or hot. I don't do it anymore as I became acquainted with the inner workings of the right front burner of our hob, but the safe, if time-consuming, way of doing the sabayon is in a Bain Marie/double boiler – as one does when melting chocolate.

A pro tip is when anything goes wrong with the sabayon (before adding the butter) such as when it splits or heads for scrambled egg, add another egg yolk and whisk vigorously. That often recovers the situation.

Another hot tip is to clarify the butter, which reduces the risk of splitting when adding the butter. Google is your friend, but the idea is to get rid of the water and the ghee in the butter before mixing it into the sabayon.

Let's put a hollandaise workshop on the agenda for our next get-together.

All hail the egg! MY TWIDDLY BITS!

W

What About Proficiency?

Five-up. Father is in control with Mother tucked tightly in behind. Three kids each perched in their space, riding along. This family is heading to the market on their 150cc Hero Honda two-wheeler. Along the way, they'll survive the bustle between hundreds of other scooters, trucks, cars, horse-carts and animals all charging to get to the next congested intersection. Located in every major city, this is one of India's innumerable Auto Anthills of propelled chaos.

Driving in India requires skills and reaction speeds not easily found in other countries. Nose-to-nose congestion does not allow time for conscious thought about options. Safe driving depends on skill plus speed of action with minimum to no error. This illustrates proficiency: the 'critical relationship between a competence' – in this case driving, 'and the speed at which it can be executed without error'. This can be neatly expressed as:

$$P = C \times S - E$$

P = Proficiency; C = Competences; S = Speed; E = Error

Note: This is not a mathematical formula or equation.

Competences make no sense without linking them to proficiency. A law enforcement officer does not have the luxury of time when confronted by an arms-bearing assailant.

Our safety and well-being in many facets of life depend on the proficiency of others who in turn may depend on our proficiency. The logistics chain that ensures the timely availability of our food supply is a modern marvel of proficiency. The prevention of nuclear war rests on among many factors, the embedded proficiency of decision-makers in command centres across the globe.

Our leadership intervention serves no purpose after the match has been lost. Appropriate pre-emptive leadership action takes proficiency to the next level. There is anticipation which provides a speed advantage, and reduction in the risk of error. A teacher who arranges therapy for a needy student before they collapse into depression. The national leader supports actions to mitigate climate change before a global tipping of disaster is reached.

Paradoxically, proficiency even with considerable competence, can also be counter-productive. An unhealthy emphasis on speed risks losing sight of people moving at a lesser pace; perhaps our family, colleagues, the ill and ageing. We may forget that good work takes time – time that speed may not allow. Loving relationships blossom as does creativity, with time.

Leaders who have no time to listen, and parents who have no time to play, risk losing the trust that depends so much on time.

Proficiency does not come from proficiency. Fluency and speed do not of themselves build more fluency and greater speed. Proficiency is a consequence of ongoing learning with regular practice and the elimination of errors. Worthy outcomes are achieved by paying attention to the things that matter and by combining urgency with patience and care.

82 LeadingMatters

Crafting Your Competence Framework

Competence frameworks provide a record – a summary – of the competences, and their underlying parts we regard as relevant to our work and personal deployment. They serve as predictive models for effective performance and personal development. I've already stressed that every person, with no exceptions, should have a competence framework – no matter how basic – linked to their current phase in life. Our knowledge and skill requirements at age 40, will differ from those we needed at age 17. Year 67 will differ from 40, and so on.

By implication, competence frameworks are personal, dynamic and contextually bound. They distinguish between our technical/functional competences and our personal competences (life skills) There are multiple examples of research-based competence frameworks and models on the web. They are aggregations of what the researchers consider as definitive norms within specified contexts. Like balance sheets, they represent snapshots of capacity – regarded as causally relevant to effective performance – at a point in time.

I've seen hundreds of competence frameworks drowned in detail based on naïve attempts to define every part to perfection. Frameworks of this nature become a burden to maintain, and easily fall into disuse. Apply the 80/20 Pareto Principle: What are the most fundamental aspects of your competences that will enable the majority of what you do?

Diagram 12: Example of Technical/Functional and Personal Competences

Examples: Technical/ Functional	Examples: Personal (Life Skills)
• Engineering	• Conceptual thinking
• Accounting	• Problem-solving
• Carpentry	• Leading
• Horticulture	• Interpersonal
• Rock mechanics	• Relational
• Marketing	• Managing
• Sales	• Collaboration and teamwork
• Film-making	• Personal mastery
• And so on	• And so on

There should be a 'light, breezy' touch to them, devoid of heavy bureaucratic, sterile language. Compiling a framework is a creative process. We should want to share them, learn from them and advance using the holistic perspectives they offer.

The level of detail included in a competence framework is a matter of personal choice. There are absolutely no hard and fast rules, except the common sense of having sufficient detail to be useful, rather than too little.

The example on the next page is what it is, an example not a one-size-fits-all prescription. It includes eight competences with statements of the capacity they should enable. A customised version may have fewer competences or perhaps a few more. I recommend no more than ten. You could combine a few and change the capacities depending on your context, tasks and priorities.

The beauty and frankly sheer joy of such a framework, which, like a great music score, brings the whole piece together, allows us to focus sharply on the capacities that really matter. We can search for and include our uniquely differentiating Twiddly Bits – those personal capacities that not only allow us to meet standards, but to exceed them.

We can test our knowledge. We can plan our development. Do we know what the primary thinking skills are in competence number two on the opposite page? How can we improve our thinking if we don't? They are listed at the end of the example on page 91.

Example of eight generic personal competences

1. Personal mastery (Who we are – identity and independence.)

What we stand for, our capacity to renew, and remain connected to the realities of self, and those around us – ultimately to function, and deploy effectively at a personal level.

This provides the capacity to:

- **Recognise** the systemic relationship between **structures**, **actions**, and **results** which in turn drive **structures** (S-A-R-S)
- **Maintain** self-awareness and intra-personal cognition
- **Develop** a repertoire of skills and behaviours that are contextually relevant
- **Accumulate** and apply relevant experience
- **Make** and sustain our own life choices
- **Select** and express substantive values
- **Use** and where necessary eliminate routines and habits
- **Nurture** your well-being – psychological, emotional, spiritual, physical and financial
- **Learn,** unlearn and relearn – life-long

A Checklist for Leading and Leadership

- **Define and craft** 'Who we choose to be' as a foundational piece for our character and personality
- **Trust** yourself and others with vulnerability

2. Conceptual thinking and reasoning (How we think.)

Our sheer 'brain power' and the degree to which we can use it to develop insight, meaning, and comprehension; Conceptualise.

This provides the capacity to:

- **Apply** primary thinking
- **Use** all our intelligences
- **Apply** different styles of thinking
- **Separate** important from unimportant
- **Conceptualise** models, theories, and possibilities
- **Apply** logic and reasoning
- **Recall**, reference, and apply perspective
- **Recognise** systemic relationships
- **Hold** contending views, especially where they challenge our personal beliefs
- **Embrace** curiosity and practice enquiry

3. Analytical, diagnostic and problem-solving (How we understand, and resolve things.)

The processes we use, and apply to gather information, extract meaning, and reach conclusions upon which we and others can act.

This provides the capacity to:

- **Apply** analytical tools including basic statistics to define problems
- **Follow** structured approaches to problem-solving including the use of web-based application tools
- **Separate** problem causes from symptoms
- **Resist** jumping to conclusions
- **Understand** the inherent errors in underestimating lead times required for realistic action implementation
- **Complete** basic cost-to-benefit evaluations
- **Complete** basic risk assessments especially those related to unintended consequences of well-intended actions
- **Identify** and eliminate errors in your thinking

4. Managing (How we create structure, process, and system.)

Our capacity to determine what needs to be done, setting up the structure(s) to get it done and ensuring completion

This provides the capacity to:

- **Formulate** objectives – short, medium, and long term
- **Define** tasks, standards, and deadlines
- **Prepare** structured plans
- **Establish** basic policies and procedures only when absolutely necessary
- **Organise** work into logical groupings
- **Delegate** work (responsibilities) and create accountability (obligations).

- **Embed** the ethos of completed staff work
- **Clarify** line-staff relationships
- **Establish** fit-for-purpose controls with linkages to plan with timeous reporting
- **Establish** high levels of self-control

5. Interpersonal, communication and presentation (How we relate, interact and project.)

Our capacity to establish credibility, predict the impact of our behaviour, and adjust our behaviour for differing situations.

This provides the capacity to:

- **Be** in touch with our context
- **Establish** and maintain lasting relationships
- **Present** ourselves in an honest manner
- **Balance** attention to self with attention to others
- **Engage** as an equal (non submissive) in interactions with others
- **Apply** communication 'skill sets' such as the Rackham interactive communication behaviours, in customised ways (not ritualistically)
- **Recognise** influencing styles, and adjust own style as required
- **Deal** with conflict, rejection, embarrassment, and personal attacks
- **Apply** basic group handling and facilitation skills

- **Prepare** and, deliver presentations with or without audio-visual support
- **Address** small to medium size audiences
- **Speak** spontaneously (without prior warning) on subjects especially those on which we are knowledgeable
- **Challenge** dysfunctionality, wrongdoing, and evil
- **Invite** and, provide feedback on behaviour, conduct, and performance

6. Collaboration and teamwork (How we add value including synergy in groups.)

Our capacity to follow, lead, generate and draw on others for mutual benefit

This provides the capacity to:

- **Distinguish** between groups and integrated, cohesive teams
- **Clarify** roles and working relationships in groups and teams
- **Build** synergy (1+1>2)
- **Know** when to lead, and when to follow in a team
- **Provide** leadership – formally or informally – including facilitating discussions, and tasks
- **Facilitate** team development through recognised stages
- **Chair** meetings
- **Challenge** dysfunctionality
- **Terminate** and/or leave the team when its mission has been completed

A Checklist for Leading and Leadership

7. Creativity and innovation (How we generate and convert ideas to realities.)

Our capacity to spot and/or generate novel ideas, assess their value, and where justified, move them along the innovation chain to fruition.

This provides the capacity to:

- **Accept** without qualification, that creativity is not limited to art, and that every person can with application, be creative
- **Spot** ideas, and opportunities
- **Apply** multiple techniques to generate our own original ideas
- **Have** the courage of our convictions to pursue ideas, and opportunities we believe have merit
- **Explain** the significant difference between creativity and innovation
- **Apply** skill, patience, and persistence in converting worthwhile ideas into worthwhile outcomes
- **Draw** on the help of others as may be required in both the process of creativity, and innovation
- **Map** innovation processes
- **Secure** sponsors for innovations.
- **Enjoy** the energy, and satisfaction that are integral parts of creativity, and innovation

8. Leading (How you influence others by default or design)

How we establish, and exercise authority, and the example we set. How we distinguish reality from imagination, determine direction, mobilise, and achieve results through the efforts of other people.

This provides the capacity to:

- **Nurture**, and pursue personal mastery as the foundation for leading and leadership
- **Take charge** – step up – assert where required – provide leadership
- **Remain** contextually connected, and relevant
- **Respond** appropriately, both proactively, and spontaneously, to changes in our context
- **Secure** resources
- **Partner** with people to pursue goals, and undertake tasks they would typically not have undertaken had you not intervened
- **Craft** conditions that will help others succeed both personally and professionally
- **Deliver** results that have impact and relevance
- **Learn,** share and, adapt

Thinking skills, for the record: **See** and recognise patterns, **Apply** memory recall, **Direct** attention, **Explore** experience, **Gather** and apply knowledge, **Know** when and how to deal with situations, and **Transfer** what we know to other situations.

This is not Alice in Wonderland stuff. The capacities in the bullet lists are pragmatic capacities that will equip us for work, and life. We acquire them with practice. If you disagree with any of the capacities listed in the example, leave them out. Add other parts

A Checklist for Leading and Leadership

you believe are essential. Not everything, just essential. Reduce the example by 50% if that works for you. The framework is a listing over many years. It is not a one-size-fits-all prescription.

The key is to remember why having a personal competence framework is important. It is a common practice for academics and other professions to build knowledge maps. They are valuable and have their place, but are not a substitute for holistic competence frameworks which integrate all the aspects of **enabling capacity**.

Earlier in the book I mentioned the critical thinking errors Rolf Dobelli listed and that my trusted friend could not fully recall. In competence number 3 above, I've included 'to identify and eliminate errors in our thinking'. Well, how can we do that if we don't know what the most critical errors are? We can't fix something we don't even realise exists and may be broken.

Compiling a personal competence framework is a work in progress requiring regular updates to ensure we are in sync with our circumstances. It may require minor adjustments or major changes. Our competences allow us to deal with both possibilities.

Can we be successful and lead a fulfilling and meaningful life without a personal competence framework? Yes of course we can and many people do.

There are pros and cons to both approaches.

Having a personal competence framework provides perspective, purpose and structure. Like any valuable routine, it takes time to develop and maintain. Working without one is comparable to flying without instruments in a crowded sky. That's feasible but not sensible.

When it comes to your life, you carry the consequences of your choices. When it comes to leading, the consequences of our poor choices are carried by others. They deserve the best of us and having a personal competence framework helps us achieve exactly that: our best.

Why would anyone settle for less?

OUR FUNCTIONAL COMPETENCES

Work as Meaning and Identity

Years before leaving school, students agonise about their future work careers. Even before that, we fantasise about the jobs that will provide our ticket to security and advancement. The functional/technical work we choose or stumble into is central to our identity.

The guidance we receive from the influential people in our life – our leaders by design, and default, in making our choice can, and frequently does impact on us for life. Functional/technical work carries a status that affects our esteem and sense of self-worth. Work is also a pathway to social mobility and socioeconomic means.

We shape our work, and it in turn shapes us. Our places of work are theatres of social interaction where networks and friendships are forged. What we do narrates the story of who we are, and with time, leaves a legacy of who we were.

Our functional/technical work is serious stuff. It makes sense to map a competence framework but no sense to produce reams of pages that duplicate what we already have in textbooks, trainer manuals, and other materials collected along the way.

Preparing a framework for functional/technical competences generates the same benefits as those that accrue with a framework for personal competences. The difference is that it is much easier and quicker to compile. The curricula provided by thousands of universities, technical colleges, business schools, professional bodies and governments are mind-boggling. No profound insight is required to recognise that the functional/technical competences we must master must provide the best fit for the roles, and tasks we fulfil for a living. The permutations are endless.

The American Association of Medical Colleges (AAMC) lists more than 135 medical specialities and subspecialities for aspirant physicians to pursue, and each requires a residency of between three to eight years.

Whether we are starting out as unskilled hands, pursuing employment that has a low, easy entry threshold or aiming to be a world-class scientist, the same fundamentals apply. Success will depend on our mastery of applicable functional/technical knowledge, skill fluency and adherence to the standards associated with the work.

All functional/technical work starts with some form of input followed by processing and outputs. The input, processing and output parts may be straightforward in nature or comprise hundreds of sub-parts along an extended value chain.

Selling in its most basic format starts with understanding customer needs, provisioning for them and closing the sale. Those would be the skills to master as a sales associate. The sales manager escalates to competences in market and competitor analysis, forecasting trends, and demand, sourcing suppliers, determining ranges, buying, logistics, merchandising, staff training, sales, cross-selling, customer service and after-sales care.

Amongst zillions of possibilities, engineers have technology forecasts. Architects have ecological impact issues. Tradespeople have automation and basic business issues. Nurses have dreaded diseases to contend with. The bottom line is the same for everybody: Master the fundamentals – the core of the function/technology upon which sound careers are built. Evolve from there.

Leaders start with the end in mind, not the means. The same principle applies to aspirant bakers, and small family business owners, to budding neurosurgeons and global corporations. Competence precedes delivery.

Average precedes excellence and that precedes mastery.

In each case, advancement – apart from luck – depends on acquiring the competences that are causally related to effective performance. Not just all or just any competences. What are the critical few which absolutely must be mastered?

For some professions that means knowing a lot about a little while in others, it may mean knowing a little about a lot. Irrespective, compiling your own competence framework will be a differentiator. Functional/technical mastery as with all competences, is contextually bound.

Our personal competences amplify whatever we undertake with our functional/technical competences.

Chinese Rice Farmers Versus SpaceX Engineers

The earliest cultivation of rice in China dates back at least 7000 years to the banks of the Yangtze River. It remains a labour-intensive operation despite government-sponsored modernisation, sophisticated irrigation systems and the magnificent terraced rice fields that have maximised arable land. For the Chinese rice workers, who have shaped the country's cultural heritage over thousands of centuries, the functional mastery is both sophisticated and humbling. Their lifestyles are modest yet proudly enabling.

Space Exploration Technologies Corp., which trades as SpaceX, is an American spacecraft manufacturer, launch service provider and satellite communications company. Founded in 2002, it has gone from zero to a global hero in just over twenty years. Their list of technological breakthroughs, willingness to risk and learning from failure, is already legendary. In 2023, their Starlink Program – one of many, comprised more than 4300 small satellites in orbit around the Earth.

IN SUMMARY: POINTS TO PONDER

1.
Understanding competence is fundamental to human development and pivotal for leading and leadership.

2.
Every person – no exceptions – should know what competences can best contribute to their success.

3.
Competences unlock potential, and thereby create more potential.

4.
A personalised competence framework provides a roadmap into success and fulfillment.

5.
Contexts and circumstances change. We change. Competences don't change – not automatically. They change by choice and conscious effort.

6.
What would a competence framework containing only treasured "Twiddly Bits" look like?

7.
Proficiency is the high octane for competence.

8.
Superior performance requires superior competence. Context sets the standards for both.

9.
The nature of functional work can add major meaning to a person's life.

OUR PERSONAL COMPETENCES

Deciding What Matters Most

The decisions we make about the personal competences that matter most to each of us should be dynamic and evolving. They keep us in touch and relevant in an ever-changing world. People new to the opportunities that personal competences offer, can start from scratch or use generic examples such as those listed on pages 85 to 91, and others that are freely available on the web.

Seasoned campaigners who already have a resumé of valuable personal competences will benefit from calibrating and updating by using the guidelines that follow. The relative value of our competences, and the investment we make in developing them changes over time. The exponential growth in artificial intelligence based on large language models (LLMs) currently taking the world by storm, is already impacting conceptual thinking, analytical skills and communication.

The one personal competence that should be mandatory for everybody is Personal Mastery.

Personal Mastery as a Cornerstone for Leading and Life

One of the central questions about leading is always "Where do I start and how do I continue?" There are multiple options which emphasise different aspects and approaches. Only one provides the right foundation and trajectory.

While at UCLA Berkley, Professor Leo Buscaglia taught: "That without knowledge, we can only share our ignorance. Without a sense of purpose in life, we can only share apathy. Without a willingness to forgive, we can only impose our judgements. Without an honest sense of love and appreciation for self, we can only share disdain and indifference. **We simply cannot give to others what we don't have**."

Leading starts with you, and I, and each of us, at a personal level. It does not start with technique, whitewater rafting or enlightenment from falling off a horse. Leading and leadership starts with aspirational people who want to make the most of their lives, and in so doing, have more to share of the things that matter in leadership: purpose, direction, support, development, achievement and constructive engagement.

The process of leading with intent starts with competence in personal mastery. A rose by any other name, remains a rose. Call Personal Mastery whatever you like, as long as you embrace the underlying intent of personal mastery. There are no formulas, prescriptions, or religious doctrines. There are no fixed points, ideologies or rules. Those are a few things that personal mastery is not. What then is it?

Personal Mastery provides a framework which we use to shape our life, and consequently, our leadership. We forge our identity and grow our character. Identity, character and personality are not divine endowments or life-long prescriptions. They are the dynamic consequences of decisions we make, commitments we uphold, and efforts we apply – all of which become the manifesto for our leading and leadership.

Personal Mastery Unpacked

Firstly, with personal mastery, we learn to **recognise**:

- How **structures**, particularly our mindset structures, drive what we do – our actions, and the results we achieve.
- The truth and reality about ourselves, and the patterns of our life.

> **Important clarification:**
>
> ***Structure** refers to the arrangement of and relations between the parts or elements of something complex. Our mental models, paradigms, values, attitudes, beliefs, and superstitions – what we think and believe are the parts of our **mindset structure**. We can regard this as '**internal** structure' – the 'constructs and cognitions' that in part drive what we do. – our actions.*
>
> *What we do and how we behave is also influenced by '**external** structures' such as rules, and regulations, policies, contracts, cultural practices, peer pressure, physical constructs, signs, employment practices, and power dynamics. Diagram 13 provides a visual representation of this dynamic, and complex relationship.*

Diagram 13: The relationship between structures (mindset and external), actions, results and thinking

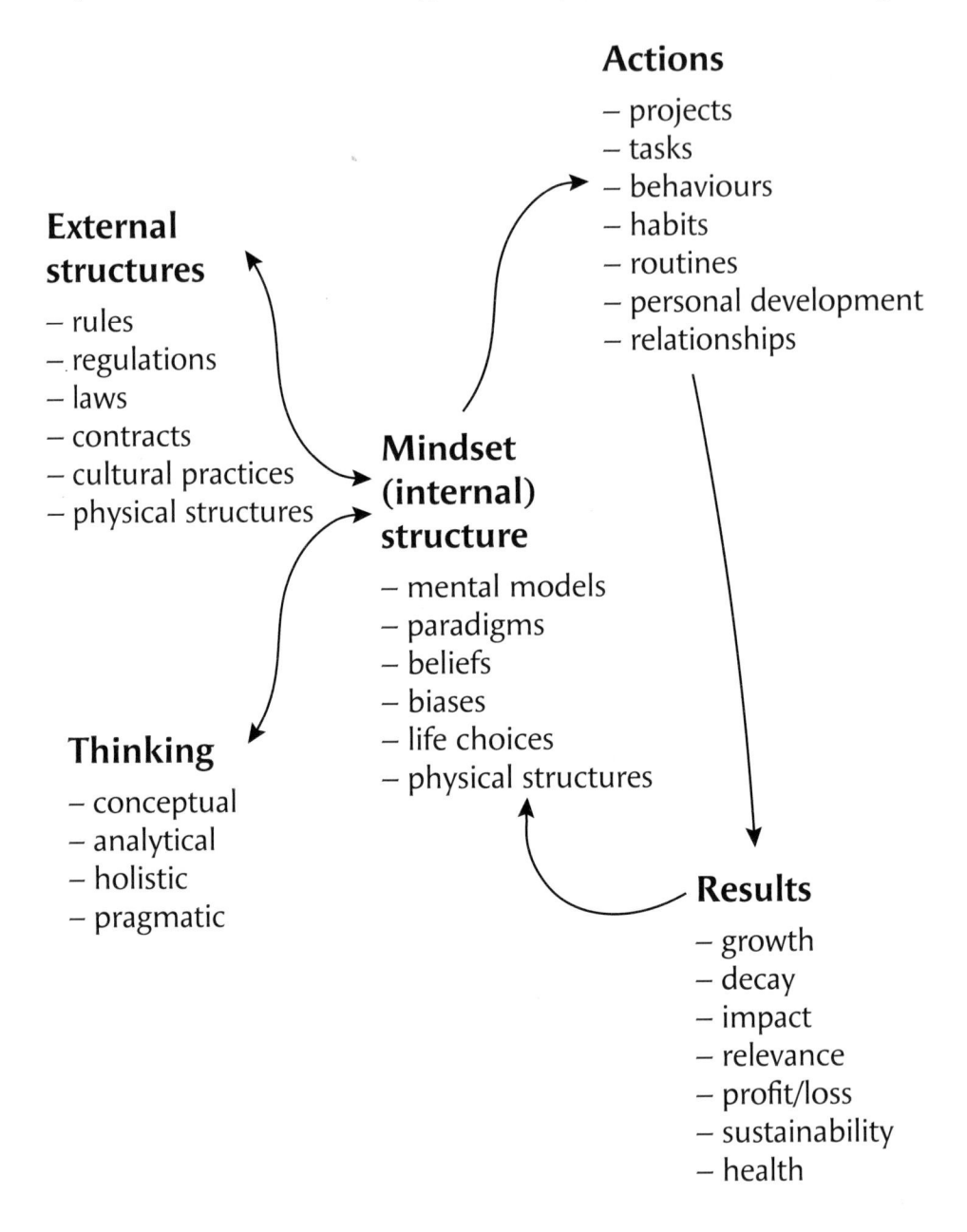

Actions
- projects
- tasks
- behaviours
- habits
- routines
- personal development
- relationships

External structures
- rules
- regulations
- laws
- contracts
- cultural practices
- physical structures

Mindset (internal) structure
- mental models
- paradigms
- beliefs
- biases
- life choices
- physical structures

Thinking
- conceptual
- analytical
- holistic
- pragmatic

Results
- growth
- decay
- impact
- relevance
- profit/loss
- sustainability
- health

Secondly, with personal mastery, we develop the **skills** and **routines** to continuously:

- Craft, and renew our **mindset (internal)** structure.
- Challenge the parts of any **external structures** that we experience as constraining or destructive.
- Shape and adjust our **behaviour, habits and routines** (how we conduct ourselves).
- **Monitor** and **pursue** our well-being (**how we achieve holistic integration**).
- Keep our **life and career goals** relevant (**what we focus on**).
- Admit and correct personal errors and deficiencies (**how we learn, renew and self-correct**).

Thirdly, the pursuit of personal mastery builds the confidence to have the **courage** of our convictions, even in the face of rejection, and embarrassment to:

- **Find** and **speak** in our own voice – be authentic; Communicate what we truly think.
- **Let go** of that which is outdated and/or no longer valid and/or not appropriate in our life.
- **Preserve** and/or adapt and/or adopt that which remains relevant and important to living a full life.

Why Is Personal Mastery So Important

- It serves the dual purpose of equipping us to craft our lives and from a leading and leadership perspective, assist others to do the same.

- Crucially, it helps us understand our 'inner world', and the power we have to shape our mindset structure.

Key Features of Mindsets

- Mindsets are maps or representations of reality. We don't have Planet Earth in our head, merely pictures, drawings and descriptions.

- There is a symbiotic relationship between mindsets and our thinking skills.

- Mindsets are constructed on a collection of facts, part facts with many inferences, inferences on inferences, assumptions, prejudices, and biases.

- They are based on education and experience – our own and that of others. The when, where and recency of those sources are critical in determining relevance and accuracy.

- Mindsets influence our focus – so-called selective attention, and what we retain – so-called selective retention which typically re-enforces what we already believe, and rejects what we don't. This can be beneficial and destructive.

- Mindsets are mega sources of self-empowering energy and self-destructing beliefs. That can be an either-or scenario and even operate simultaneously. A person can be highly motivated to achieve and also feel helpless having grown up in poverty.

Given these features, it should not be hard to see that a significant amount of what we hold in our mindset is incomplete, flawed and outdated.

People proficient in personal mastery, recognise these pitfalls and adjust accordingly. Those who lack personal mastery, treat their thinking as universal truths. They offer opinions as facts. They rely on generalisations and stereotypes. They are dangerous legends in their own mind.

Diagram 14: The main components of mindset structure

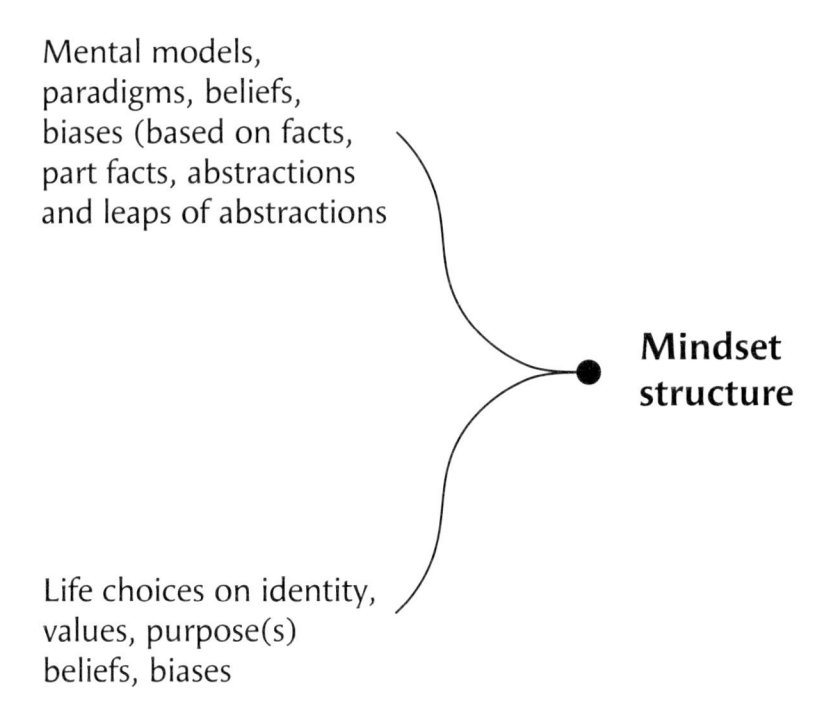

- Mental models, paradigms, beliefs, biases (based on facts, part facts, abstractions and leaps of abstractions
- Life choices on identity, values, purpose(s) beliefs, biases

→ **Mindset structure**

The table on the next page gives a small sample of how what people believed has and is changing.

Mindsets on the Move: Evolving Paradigms and Mental Models

The world is changing. Life is changing. People are changing.

Paradigm on…	Past	Present and emerging
Organising	Hierarchy is best	Network is best
Focus	First on organisation	Individual first
Work arrangements	Highly structured	Highly flexible
Product quality	Affordable best	No compromise
Work relationships	Formal	Semi-formal and informal
Status	Title and position	Contribution
Influence	Based on positional power	Mostly personal power; Do we need power
Challenge	Not seniors	Anybody, anywhere
Intimacy	Taboo subject	Open conversation
Physics	Newtonian	Quantum theory and relativity
Origins of life	Divine intervention	Divine intervention and evolutionary biology
Terrorism	Fanatic fringes	Religious, political, and left- and right-wing extremists
Life purpose	Singular	Plural
Wealth	Money-quantity	Life-quality
Career	Security	Opportunity
Leadership	Control skills and males	Life skills and everybody
Exercise	If time allows	A necessity
Family	Secondary to work	Precedence over work
Business	Local	Global – as local
Change	Reactive	Proactive
Homemaking	Female responsibility	Shared by family
Information	Sorted and filed	Googled and free flow

Paradigm on…	Past	Present and emerging
Software development	Restricted source	Open source – AI
Learning	Individuals	Communities and organisations
Competitive advantage	Size	The rate of learning, innovation and application
Strategy	Small changes over time	Rapid changes in short cycles
Economic borders	National	None – borderless world
Political power	Dedicated politicians	Career politicians, corporate money, winner takes all, interest groups
Research and development	Scientist-led and government- and corporate-funded	User-led and entrepreneur- and crowd-funded
Diets	Meat people	Cyber people
Seat of intelligence	Determined by birth	Determined by culture and curiosity
Brain functioning	Classical neural network	Living ecology of a jungle

THIS WAY UP ⬇

The Leverage for Change

Nurturing Personal Mastery is not a step-by-step, sequential process. There is no endpoint. By recognising the relationship between what we think, how we think and the actions we take – Diagram 13, page 100 – we create the opportunity for ongoing, continuous improvement.

In personal mastery, **self-awareness** is the primary lever for change. People don't just change for the sake of change. We need reasons, and there is no better source than **self-insight and ownership** – our desire to be in control of who and what we are and can yet become. Coercion and inducements can also trigger change but are poor substitutes for our free will.

The realisation that certain aspects of our behaviour may be offensive at least creates an opportunity – not a guarantee – to make corrections. Without that awareness, the likelihood of change is low to zero.

Our behaviour may be consistent with our beliefs yet still be flawed where the beliefs are flawed. The behaviour of chauvinistic males shows how prejudiced thinking leads to disrespectful behaviour. Business leaders who ignore the pollution their operations cause, reveal poor value judgement, selfish attitudes, and unacceptable conduct.

Personal Modelling

How do we move from awareness to meaningful change? Before travelling, we pack a bag or two. We consider what to include and what to leave out. Along the way, we discover new things. We decide what stays, gets added, and gets tossed. The pursuit of personal mastery works the same way.

Our 'personal bag' contains everything that represents us – mindset structure, skills, behaviours, values, habits routines, identity, and so on. Who packed our original bag when we started out? Not us. What's in the bag? How relevant and useful are the contents? How do we find out and ensure we have what we need to sustain the life we choose?

The answer is by following a straightforward, down-to-earth process of **personal modelling**. Wherever we are, whatever our age and circumstances, we can make the following four actions a routine part of our life:

Monitor and filter:
We need to think carefully about the validity and usefulness of any new data and information that crosses our path before including it in what we think and believe. We should apply the same routine about advice, and even instructions relating to how we live, work, and behave. Thoughtful people take very little for granted not because they are cynical or untrusting. On the contrary. They are discerning and refuse to be gullible to false narratives, pseudo-science and exaggerated claims.

The fact that a superstar celebrity endorses a product does not make it useful until we have clarity on the validity of the recommendation. Investors worldwide lose millions of dollars annually on fraudulent schemes. A publication on science does not make the contents scientific. The absence of facts leaves us in the realm of opinions.

Surface and make visible:
A significant amount – some argue the majority – of what we think and do occurs below a level of conscious thought. We respond spontaneously, and correctly so for fluency and continuity. The underlying facts, and assumptions upon which our views, beliefs, and mental models are based, remain invisible. As

natural as this is, it blocks updating and validation against new knowledge and practices.

By surfacing our underlying thinking – intentionally bringing it to a level of conscious thought – we get to know what is in our bag. What supports our thinking and beliefs?

Offering opinions about anything and everything is easy. Providing credible, objective facts which validate the assertions is much harder. No amount of fancy rhetoric can justify bad behaviour.

Test and validate:

With awareness, we create opportunities to test and validate our previously hidden facts and assumptions. We gain better insight into why we behave as we do. We can reflect privately on the contents of our bag and where possible, invite discussion, and support from others. They can do the same. The value of introspection and interaction of this nature far exceeds the feelings of vulnerability that are an integral part of a personal modelling process.

Adjust and celebrate:

Every correction and improvement we make to our mindset, behaviours and everything else that makes up our bag, is a victory worth celebrating. Seeing the world, and ourselves more accurately, being more skilful, and just simply moving forward toward a more fulfilling life is a cause worth pursuing.

With personal modelling, we are the artist and the creation. We can focus on any of the parts that fill our bag of self. Mindset modelling, behaviour modelling, skills modelling, values modelling, attitude modelling, habits modelling and well-being modelling are the subsets of ongoing renewal and growth. If ever there was an aphrodisiac, that must enjoy the first place.

Please keep in mind we are dealing with Personal Mastery as a cornerstone for life and leading. The more pragmatic we can be, the better. High-rise buildings are not built on generalised notions of structural engineering. The same principle applies to 'high-rise' people. There is skill in how they monitor and filter information. They have the courage to surface and make visible their underlying thinking. Vulnerability is accepted in order to test, validate and adjust.

Behaviour and Skills Modelling

Rudeness and lateness are not genetically encoded. They are bad behaviour. Single acts of conduct reveal more than just the behaviour they are displaying. When used erratically and without malicious intent, they can be forgiven. Certainly at least once. When used consistently with brazen disregard for the disrespect they impart, they should attract rebuke, not pardon.

Behaviour refers to the conduct and actions people display in response to their thoughts and feelings, and stimuli from other people. The range of possibilities is endless as the listing on the opposite page shows. Behaviour is an observable action which can be measured, quantified and characterised.

You don't have to be a behavioural psychologist or sociologist to appreciate that behaviour is the means by which we express ourselves to the world. In like fashion, our understanding of and appreciation for other people is largely based on our perceptions of their behaviour. What we observe in others, and what they observe in us, is open to a library of interpretations depending on culture, context, and content.

We learn a significant amount from the behaviour of others and competent leaders are highly tuned to modelling the behaviours they would like others to adopt.

Multiple ways to describe and classify behaviours

Verbal - Non-verbal - Passive – Aggressive

Open – Closed – Sympathetic – Empathetic

Soft – Loud – Expected – Unexpected

Warm – Cold – Appropriate – Inappropriate

Timely – Late – Neutral – Biased

Quiet – Noisy – Dull – Colourful

Direct – Indirect – Limited – Extensive

Narrow – Expansive – Introverted – Extroverted

Sensitive – Insensitive – Mannered – Abrasive

Kind – Cruel – Spontaneous – Premeditated

Egalitarian – Elitist – Respectful – Profane

Light – Heavy – Caring – Hurtful

Judgemental – Non-judgemental

Selfish – Sharing – Loving – Clinical

Worldly – Mystical – Personal choice – Prescribed

In a flash – one iteration

Over time – as patterns

Subjectively and/or objectively

Developing a behavioural repertoire is not about long lists. That's a challenge for performing artists. Our task is to ensure that the behaviours we use, are:

- Mostly appropriate for the situation. Why mostly?
- Used with fluency and confidence – proficiently;
- Consistent with our life choices;
- Authentic – not a pretentious mask;
- Useful and constructive.

Why mostly? We are not robots or single-cell amorphous blobs. As dynamic living entities with emotions and feelings, our behavioural responses will vary. Letting off steam, and showing anger can on occasion be more appropriate than a stiff-faced clinical response after being betrayed by someone you trusted. Anger would be inappropriate when screaming at the driver who just rear-ended your new auto, especially if you failed to notice they had suffered a heart attack which caused their inability to stop in time.

Most people have at some stage been involved in arguments that deteriorated into heated, personal attacks. The interaction moves from a focus on content with facts to personal attacks, and hurtful remarks.

Imagine if you or the other person could freeze the interaction to compare your behaviour in action – hurtful assertions – with your respective life choices. Would your life choices include: "I choose to hurt other people. I choose to inflict pain. I choose to not hold myself responsible for my behaviour when other people offend me."

Those are unlikely choices, yet there we go, hurting people, often repeatedly, despite the values we supposedly subscribe to. Teenagers and parents can be very abusive to each other despite

Our Personal Competences

their professed love. Is that what they choose? Displaying behaviour that wounds a so-called loved one. Similar behaviour is fairly common in many adult relationships. The lever for change is to:

- Recognise the gaps between what we preach and what we practice.
- Take responsibility for your behaviour and avoid blaming others. 'You make me so angry' is a rubbish assertion because nobody can make you angry without your permission.

In the main, people choose to be positive and productive. Yet surprisingly, large numbers of people behave in ways that are completely opposite. They attend meetings they regard as a waste of time. When invited to make suggestions during the meeting, they make no contribution. They complain about the meeting to people who have no authority to change the meeting.

Their behaviour is inconsistent with their life choices; they fail to intervene with leadership that can correct the situation, and they blame others without even remotely considering that they may be a part of the problem.

To freeze that meeting, to recognise your part in the problem, and to have the integrity to acknowledge the personal error, are examples of people practising Personal Mastery. The ownership creates the opportunity for correction and improvement. Denial blocks the pathway to mastery. How could that ever be a choice?

> We shape ourself to fit the world and by the world are shaped again. The visible and the invisible working together in common cause to produce the miraculous.
> David Whyte: *Crossing the Unknown Sea*, p202

"Human behaviour flows from three main sources: desire, emotion, and knowledge." PLATO

"Behaviour is the mirror in which everyone shows their image." GOETHE

"People don't change their behaviour unless it makes a difference for them to do so." SHARON MORGEN

"Your first and foremost job as a leader is to take charge of your own energy." PETER DRUCKER

"Technique ignores the factor of magic; craftsmanship presupposes it. A journeyman, after seven years as an apprentice, will get the feel of his materials and learn what quiet miracles can be done with them. A small part of this knowledge is verbally communicable: the rest is uncommunicable, except to fellow craftsman who already possess it." THE POET ROBERT GRAVES, SPEAKING AT OXFORD IN 1962

"The winds and the waves are always on the side of the ablest navigator." EDWARD GIBBON

"Skill to do comes of doing." RALPH WALDO EMERSON

"Continuous improvement is better than delayed perfection." MARK TWAIN

"Skill is the unified force of experience, intellect and passion." JOHN RUSKIN

"The only way to do great work is to love what you do." STEVE JOBS

Skills are combinations of behaviours, knowledge and experience that enable us to complete specific tasks and respond to situations.

They are dynamic and can change over time. Skills are not single-point capabilities. As with competences as a whole, the users' level of proficiency is important. This could range from low to high proficiency, or poorly developed to highly developed and any other anchors you may find helpful. Auto drivers are not equally skilled. Not every school teacher can direct the school's choir. Many leaders lack the skills needed for effective coaching.

Diagram 15: Verbal behaviours contributing to interpersonal skill

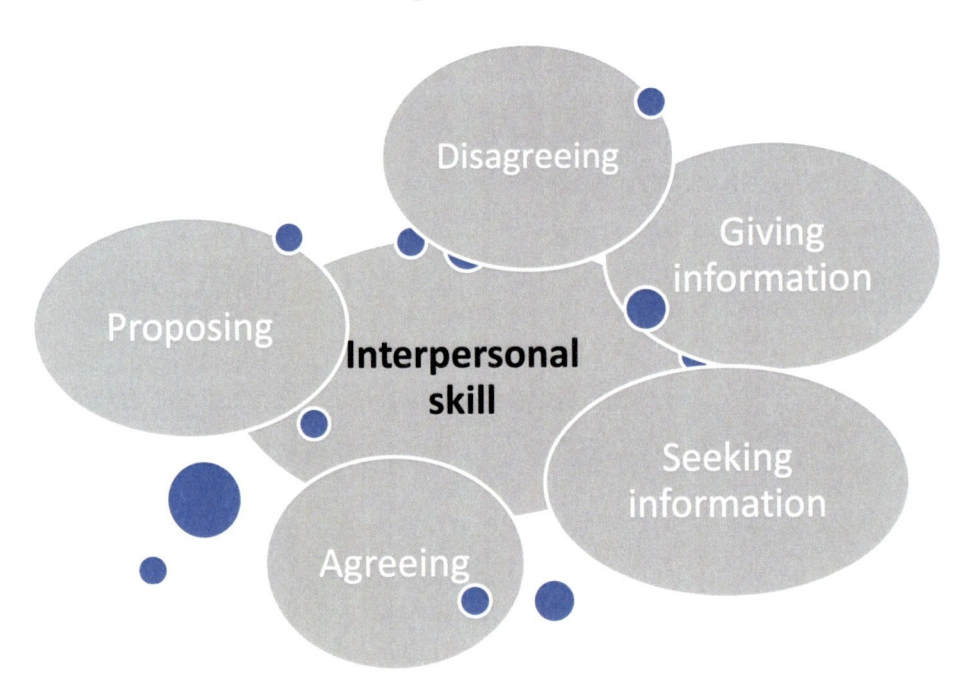

- Disagreeing
- Giving information
- Proposing
- **Interpersonal skill**
- Seeking information
- Agreeing

Diagram 16: Dancing skills contributing to other skill sets

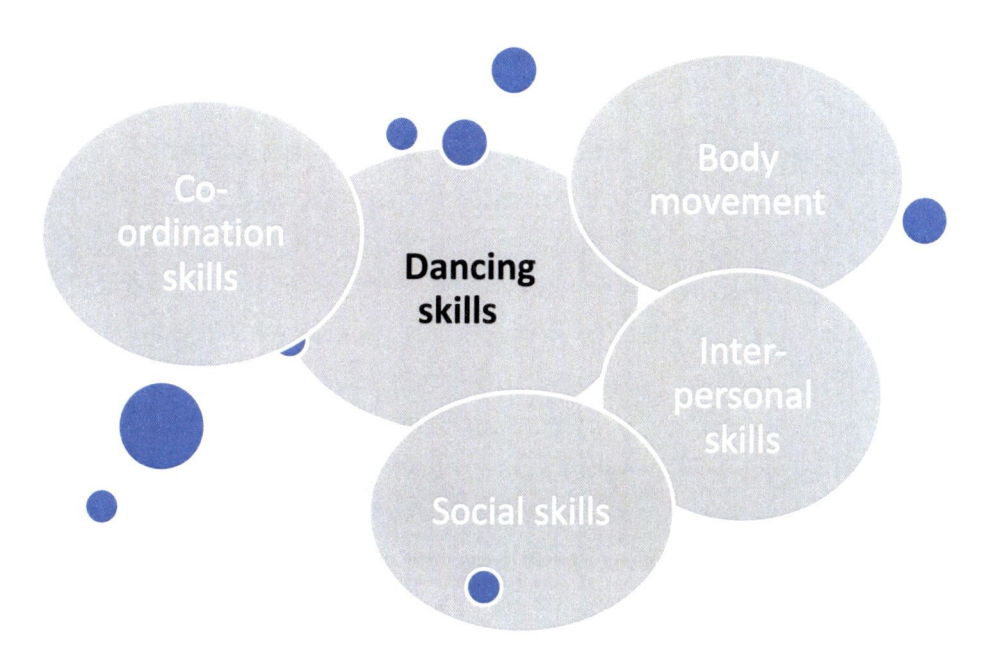

- Co-ordination skills
- Dancing skills
- Body movement
- Inter-personal skills
- Social skills

Skills are typically classified as:

- Soft skills that enable us to interact with others and respond to social situations. Examples include presentation of self, challenging, etiquette, and romancing.

- Technical skills related to specific functional and technical tasks, professions, and industries. Examples include accounting, law enforcement, programming and nursing.

- Hybrid skills that we can use in both technical and soft situations. Examples include problem-solving, perception and pattern recognition and collaboration.

- Basic vs advanced skills, depending on their complexity and the time it takes to develop proficiency.

- Cognitive vs motor skills, the former requiring mostly mental processing, and the latter, mostly physical activity.

The early selection and development of desirable skills attract the benefit of compounded learning – the accumulation of knowledge, experience and confidence that build on themselves.

Can you still recall the formula for compound interest? You learnt this fundamental piece of knowledge at school. Although mostly associated with finance, the benefits of compound interest accrue in the same way for knowledge, experience and skills. This is by far one of the most powerful forces in the universe.

We see abundant evidence of this compounding effect in so-called legacy skills – where craftspeople have accumulated their knowledge, experience and mastery passed down from generation to generation. Economist Brian Arthur describes this 'deep craft', as 'a more profound and stickier expertise'. In Personal Mastery as in leading and leadership, we must recognise that skills are not just skills.

Ian Goldin and Chris Kuturna are almost poetic as they write about the tacit understanding that skilled practitioners acquire and exhibit in contemporary society. For them: "Our science, technology and systems are far more advanced. Whether you mix music, write code and engineer robots or estimate economic growth, the mysteries at the leading edge are deeper and take longer to learn, the range of disciplines that must come together to make a breakthrough is wider, and the universe of possible solutions is so vast that only a well-honed intuition can help you on a productive path. All this multiplies the unspoken knowing that separate the able from the adept." *The Age of Discovery*, p245.

Formula for compound interest

A = P (1 + r/n)^{nt}

- A is the future/final balance including interest
- P is the amount of the initial investment
- r is the annual interest rate in decimal terms
- n is the number of times the interest is compounded per year
- t is the time/period the money is invested.

Some of the benefits that accrue from compound interest are:

- Higher returns
- Wealth accumulation – financial, intellectual, emotional, spiritual
- Risk mitigation
- Optimisation of resources
- Greater breadth and depth of knowledge, skills, experience, etc.
- Sharper insights and perspective
- Sounder judgement with improved decision-making
- Seamless integration of your 'Twiddly Bits'.

Actions to develop your repertoire of skills

Observe and learn	Pay attention.
	Identify role models who are respected for their skills in varying circumstances. Learn to spot the differences, often barely discernible, between their skills and those who just busk and blunder along. Films, interviews, commencement speeches and documentaries can be great sources of learning where you view them as study material and not just entertainment.
Take stock	Cherish any feedback and data you can collect – no matter how critical, on the range and proficiency of your skills.
	Use the data from self-assessments, practical tests, and feedback to identify strengths you can build on, and gaps you may need to fill. Competent, experienced coaches and mentors can be very valuable in this regard.
Develop	Prioritise and practice, repeatedly, until you achieve high proficiency. Practice is the pathway to mastery. It can be boring, but it's necessary. Scientists mostly hate it.
Renew and update	Professionals – doctors, engineers and many others, are required by law to complete regular re-training and updating. We all should do the same.

Values and Attitudes: No Easy Matter

Values or if you prefer, **principles** are deeply held beliefs about what we regard as morally right and wrong. They guide our decision-making and behaviour by setting boundaries and standards for our conduct. By implication, they are an integral part of our mindset structure with the caveat, 'when adhered to' because that is frequently not the case.

There are daily reports across the globe of leaders in business, politics, religion and humanitarian aid who are abusive, corrupt and expedient despite the virtuous images they like to project. I'm sure you could name several especially if you reflect on the 2024 USA Presidential Election.

Values serve as permissions, and embargoes, green and red flags. All are constructs, drawn mostly from doctrines, philosophies, and religions which initially shape our early upbringing. We adopt them from our cultural experiences and the people we regard as significant.

Therein is the luck of the draw. Our early programming has a profound influence on our life. It can be a launch pad for intrinsic meaning or a ticket to life-long misery if left untouched. Values have for centuries, been at the root of both amazing good and horrendous evil. In ancient, medieval and early modern societies, torture – inflicting physical pain, and suffering on people – was regarded as legally and morally acceptable. The outcomes of those values would not have been pleasant for people on the receiving end.

The Atlantic slave trade (fifteenth to nineteenth centuries), the Holocaust during World War II, the Rape of Nanking (Nanjing massacre: 1937-1938), the forced removal of Native American tribes in the south-eastern United States in the 1800s, the Khmer Rouge Regime in Cambodia, the mass slaughter of an estimated 800,000 to 1 million Tutsis in the Rwandan Genocide (1994) and the horrors of the Gaza War (from 2023) between Israel and Hamas, are examples of how evil can be embedded in the minds of deranged leaders.

We must each choose the principles we wish to live by. A few criteria to consider when making your choice, are:

- How constructive, positive and helpful are my values?
- What sense of wholeness and fulfilment do they create?
- How do they reflect my identity – how I want to be known?

Selecting a handful of values that can be remembered, and applied with consistency is far more beneficial than a long list that may look impressive, but creates hubris instead of focussed clarity.

Here are a few options:

- Self-discipline
- Integrity
- Reliability
- Respect your body and mind
- A work ethic
- Punctuality (perhaps a part of reliability)
- Life-long learning
- Love
- Loyalty
- Fairness
- Family first
- Forgiveness
- Merit
- Drive and aspiration
- Respect – social: self and others
- Compassion and caring
- A sense of fun and playfulness
- A sense of urgency and intensity
- Intolerance for bigotry and discrimination

Attitudes are the feelings, dispositions, opinions and judgements we hold about people, events, ideas, situations and issues. Like values, they are constructs which are shaped and change over time. We display them through our verbal and non-verbal behaviour.

Once embedded, they generate default responses without conscious thought. While that is regarded as normal behaviour, a natural, spontaneous response does not automatically equal an appropriate response. Attitudes can be and often are, tainted with biases, prejudices, misunderstandings and a litany of other such deficiencies. They are not fixed points, and we can flex them according to choice.

John (not his real name), was an executive-level manager at a National Research Centre. He held a PhD and MBA. During a feedback session following a 3-day leadership assessment workshop, his attention was drawn to his excessively aggressive attitude and behaviour. "That's not an issue," he responded. "I've always been like that. My staff know I'm temperamental and moody. I grew up in an abusive home where my father regularly beat my mother. I've been through three marriages. I have an enviable record of achievement. What more can this organisation and the staff expect? I'm 57 years old and can't change who I am."

This true account is a classic tale of everyday events in families, schools and organisations across the globe. Narcissistic attitudes that "I'm ok, can't and won't change; this is who I am; I've always been like this," are completely warped.

Shortly after receiving his detailed assessment, and the resignation of his entire team, he did change. He changed at age 57 to become a role model of what can be achieved when an individual accepts responsibility for their conduct. No more projections and rationalisations. The realisation that a small change in attitude, and a little tweak in behaviour with ownership of choice, caused an individual to transform his life. That change in turn positively impacted a larger circle of people who in turn influenced others.

Our personal mastery matters as does the impact it has on the quality of our leadership. The following is a list of attitudes that can range from high to low depending on our choices and level of development.

Our Personal Competences

- Constructive to destructive
- Helpful to unhelpful
- Engaging to indifferent
- Positive to neutral to negative
- Warm to cold
- Open to closed
- Passive to aggressive
- Trusting to circumspect
- Accommodating to selfish
- Sharing to selfish
- Enlightening to morbid

Easy Words: Tough Realities

The Spanish newspaper *Marca* reported on 27 August 2023 that a staggering 11,000 runners, out of a 30,000-person field, were disqualified after it was discovered they had crossed the finish line without having completed the full course for the Mexico City Marathon.

36.7 percent had cheated. Do you think they all belong to a dark web of crime or rather, are known to the world as respectable citizens, moms and dads, teachers, clergy and trustworthy business folk? It would be insightful to hear them explain the contradictions between the values they espouse and the values they practice.

Although it may seem **challenging, choosing values and attitudes is relatively easy. Living by them – the part that counts – presents the tough reality**. Closing that gap with discipline and firm resolve is a building block in Personal Mastery. Eliminating gaps is a prerequisite for people who wish to lead with integrity. In his brilliant 2017 book, *Principles*, Ray Dalio explains how to 'embrace reality and deal with it'. He advocates trusting in radical truth and radical transparency. He should know. Over a forty-year period, he built Bridgewater into the fifth most important private company in the USA. His gracious acknowledgement of the people who shared that journey and his testimony to many others who embrace the principle of radical truth and transparency is a lesson for any person seeking truthful expression of their values and attitudes.

Otherwise, why bother?

The Law and the Outlaw

"To preserve a sense of freedom even in the midst of rules and regulations is to preserve a part of our identities free from the strictures and responsibilities of success, career and corporation. The measure of our continuing individuality in any work is the refusal to be swallowed by our goals, our ambitions, or our company no matter how marvelous they may be. In order to live happily within outer laws, we must have a part of us that goes its own way, that is blessedly outlaw no matter the outward conditions or rewards."

David Whyte: *Crossing the Unknown Sea*, p 156

Habits and Routines: Elevators Up – Greasy Poles Down

The subject of habits and routines has been covered by hundreds of books, research papers, popular articles, podcasts, videos and TED Talks. Adding more commentary would, in my considered opinion, be a waste of time which is the very opposite of what habits and routines are supposed to do.

Habits and routines are frequently used as 'clickbait' on the internet when combined with hooks such as:

- The 37 Habits of Successful People.
- The 19 Daily Habits for Healthy Living.
- The 14 Habits of Great Leaders.
- The Life-long Routines of Buddhist Monks.
- The three secret routines that will revolutionise your life.

As tempting as they may sound, they should never be taken for granted or followed without consideration of your personal needs and context. What works for Mishra may be disastrous for you. What works for 200 senior leaders in a steel mill, could be a kiss of death for the top 12 creatives in an advertising agency, and vice versa. Customisation for relevance and impact is the modelling to apply. Avoiding formulas, and simplistic generalisations that promise quick fixes and easy solutions is a great habit. Habits and routines are intended to:

- Provide effective – tested, refined and appropriate responses to recurring events and situations that work for you.
- Eliminate erratic, inconsistent behaviour and actions.
- Reduce/eliminate errors and wasteful efforts.

- Save time, energy and resources

Their importance is a given. Their value is not. Bad habits establish a treadmill of errors, which by the nature of habits and routines, easily remain out of sight. Poor eating, substance abuse, submissiveness and overspending are not worthwhile routines. We need to figure out what works best for us. A handy approach is to make a list of your most important habits and routines and then to review them on a regular – at least half-yearly – basis. It helps to apply the 80-20 Pareto Principle to identify those habits and routines, the smaller 20% we use in response to the larger 80% of the everyday events we deal with.

They can be conveniently arranged in a matrix that groups them into daily, weekly, monthly, quarterly, half-yearly and annual recurring events/actions, according to the focus or nature of the events/actions. Examples include recreation, family, learning, work – diary, emails, record-keeping, networks, reporting and planning. See Diagrams 17 and 18 on the next pages for examples.

There are many standard templates that are freely available on the internet. Diagrams 17 and 18 are examples of a customised planner designed in response to the following questions:

- "How can I as a matter of routine, match, and monitor my weekly planning with my life priorities?"
- "What planning routine will help achieve a standard of 100% reliability?"

A regular review identifies gaps and eliminates mindless carryover. The process is similar to the one we used for mental modelling in order to 'clean up' the underlying structures driving our actions and behaviour.

Diagram 17: Example of customised weekly planner – front page

Weekly Planner and Log		My game changers for the year		Weight goal: Kgs by	Last month's actual:
WE: /52		#1 #2 #3		KM goal this week:	Last week's actual:

My Priorities	Mon	Tues	Wed	Thurs	Fri	Sat	Sun
Important + Urgent							
Urgent							
Important							
Learning log							
Exercise							
Insights, ideas, and resources							
Family and Friends							
Investment and Savings							

Diagram 18: Example of customised weekly planner – rear page

Urgent and important	Important	Ongoing maintenance	Reminders
To do: Daily routine #1. Create value: #2. Work assignments: #3. Personal projects • • • #4. Learn something #5. Clear mailbox **To do: Saturday routine** • Filling • Diary update **To do: Set dates** • 10th • Last Sat month: Accounts **My Mondays** • Carpe Diem: • Discovery: **Wildcard – Test the Boundaries** •	**Active Projects** • **To call:** •	**Personal** • Filing system – Stacks • Great Graphics – examples • Investment and savings • Learning notes • Musings and Power Questions (PQs) • Personal development plan (PDP) • Health Plan **Project ideas** •	**Shopping** **DIY – 'Bird by Bird'** • **Planning dates:** • *Vacations* **Personal Manifesto Ideas** *Find and engage your network and offer them 'things' that enrich their life* *Work with the transitional paradigms of brand and competences* *Go to the Edge – Onlyness* *Confronting today's truth beats tomorrow's cover-up* *Making a profit entails taking a risk* *Work with partners* *Culture trumps strategy every time* *Being the best requires discipline and focus* *Steve: Create incredible things people want* *What's your appetite for risk*

Our Personal Competences

Monitor, and filter; Surface, and make visible; Test, and validate; Adjust, and celebrate.

Inviting critique from others is always valuable.

Being brutally honest with ourselves is not negotiable. A great place to start is with the elimination of bad habits such as interrupting people when they are speaking. Apologising beforehand with 'I'm sorry to interrupt' does not make the interruption acceptable. Fiddling with a mobile phone while attending a meeting is a terrible habit which may even be quite disrespectful. People fail to recognise that raising their voices to bully or intimidate people is a form of verbal violence. Belittling people, being abusive towards others because of their life choices and disrespecting socially accepted norms, are distasteful habits.

Sloppy verbal mannerisms reflect a disconnect from reality. People fail to hear what they are saying, how they are saying it, and the impact it has on others. "Like I was saying, we kind of like to use certain words routinely, like it doesn't matter whether it adds anything to what we are saying, which is like saying, we like to fail to notice our bad habits, like how people experience us or not. Ok, right, I get it. Ok."

These examples are like garden weeds that can easily be cleaned out. Unfortunately, weeds grow back, and so do bad habits. Diarise a half-yearly appointment to meet with yourself to:

- Review your list of habits and routines
- Eliminate those that are unhelpful and outdated
- Refine and perhaps add to those that are useful and value-adding.

Make it a fun exercise as an integral part of your evolving personal mastery. This is not just something for youngsters and aspirant A-Leaguers to undertake. The worst offenders when it comes to entrenched bad habits, and routines are senior executives and folks who have become ossified in their thinking, and ways. It need not be so.

What Experience Teaches: The Cecil Atherstone Story

Date: 10 February 2005
Route: LHR-CPT
Time: 2055UTC
Phase: Climb
Aircraft Type: Boeing 744 Jumbo
Reg: ZS-SAY
No. of crew: 3
Position: Transition from UK into French airspace
Incident: Failure of one of the primary altimeters

Background

As air travel expanded over the years, congestion and lack of 'safe space' became an issue because the turbine engines and aircraft design required that aircraft fly as high as possible thus optimising fuel burn and speed. The problem is that at high altitudes, regular altimeters were less accurate than the new-generation altimeters. To compensate for this, at the very high cruising levels of these aircraft, the vertical separation was increased from 1000ft to 2000ft.

This meant that fewer aircraft could be accommodated at these higher levels than at lower levels. The implication was that in the highly congested airspace regions, aircraft seeking to fly at those higher levels were required to have special equipment changes made to the aircraft and that the aircrew operating in Reduced

Vertical Separation Minima airspace (RVSM) were required to undergo ongoing specialised training.

Manoeuvring in this airspace was a delicate affair requiring that a constant speed and altitude needed to be strictly adhered to at ALL times. Leaving your assigned altitude by more than 150ft was a violation. The B744 has a wingspan of 211 feet 3 inches – that is how tight it was. This is all to ensure that aircraft do not collide with each other. Our airspace was set between flight level (FL) 285 (28500ft) and FL420.

A few thousand feet from our first cruising level which would have been just into RVSM airspace I became aware that the technical status of the aircraft was not that required for RVSM airspace penetration. The aircraft climbs very rapidly, over 1000ft per minute. You may not enter the RVSM with an aircraft not suitably equipped and at the same time you may not 'level off' as there are many aircraft flying at their respective cruising levels and thus you would become a safety issue.

This type of malfunction is very subtle and its correct identification, and quick action is of paramount importance to safe flight. Solving the problem did not start when the malfunction was detected. It started much earlier when I (and other good airmen) was selected for initial pilot training. Selecting the right people is the start of safety, followed by comprehensive training, both in theory and practice, followed by matching the pilot to the task with the proper equipment.

This is an ongoing challenge throughout the operational life of an aviator. Competent pilots know their equipment and the captain of the aircraft doubly so. In order to lead, you need to display ability that comes from in-depth knowledge and associated applications to the task at hand. I maintained a small book of notes on the critical factors affecting the operation of the aircraft. I always had the book at hand and would read through it from time to time going over some of the possible scenarios that one might have to face up to.

This was not a 'read and do' book, but rather a refresher for my set of responsibilities. This is one of the many tools for reliable leadership that I had available in my career. Leadership is not instinctive, it comes from training, deep knowledge of your equipment and your crew, being aware at all times of what is going on around you in the situation, and tons of experience all of which give confidence. This is what sets up the searching mind enabling you to discard all the misinformation, thereby eliminating poor judgements because of your experience.

Competent leaders do not just happen; they are made!

As far as the said flight was concerned, we managed to avoid penetrating the RVSM airspace by obtaining a clearance for a lower level through timeous quick reaction thereby avoiding a serious incident. This is one of the many success stories which thankfully do not make the news. By contrast, hesitant leadership characterised by poor judgements and decision-making creates trouble and unwelcome news.

* * * * * * *

The benefits of experience take time to accrue. Variety provides perspective and repetition provides depth with proficiency. Not all experience is worth having or retaining. The critical question is: "How do we differentiate between experience that is valuable and that which is not?" What do you think? Please at least think about it.

Take hardship and failure. Those experiences can be both painful and energising, helpful and destructive. The value of experience, and its accumulation over time, does not reside in the experience itself. The value depends on at least two critical events. Firstly, the reliability of the insights you can draw from experiences, and secondly, the extent to which we can and do apply them.

After FedEx reportedly lost over $500 million following expansion into Europe, Fred Smith, the founder and CEO at the time, reported that although expensive, it had provided innumerable experiences of great value. A common feature of combat training is subjecting recruits to severe disruption and hardship – experiences that build mental and physical resilience. Compare that takeaway with the naïve responses from people opposed to any form of discipline and experiences that build psychological robustness.

The purposeful pursuit of experiences – insights and applications we believe will enhance our competences – is an integral part of personal mastery. Time out for a sabbatical. Getting assigned to a special project. Working as an assistant to a respected role model. Professional Internships. Experimentation. Visiting the fringes where new thinking and ideas are emerging. Tapping into the experiences of high achievers in your environment. Changing employment and job rotation.

Different contexts present different opportunities for individuals willing to take the initiative. Every step does not need to be planned or mapped, but it must be pursued with an open mind.

Leader impact is enhanced when valuable experiences are shared. That can shorten the learning curve for others and add credibility to the relationship. Experience strengthens skills and skills can add experiences.

Life invariably scatters random experiences along our path. They are at least as important as the ones we intentionally pursue. The chance encounter with a stranger. The spider bite that turns septic. The disappointing job. The vacation of a lifetime. Complex tasks you master after having first thought it would not be possible. Lifting team and organisational performances well beyond expectations. A never-ending stream of surprises and diversity – often daily – from which we can draw insights.

Experiences are the conversations we have with life and the wise go in search of those conversations. The convergence of the insights drawn from modelling mindsets, behaviours, skills and the other parts of personal mastery, shapes who we are, and can become.

Who Am 'I'? The Rocky Road to Identity

It all depends. No, seriously. Depends on whose asking, when and where they're asking, and how you are feeling at that moment, amongst multiple possibilities.

"I'm skin and bone. 97% water."

"Hi, I'm Rodney. I'm an alcoholic. I'm wasted. I'm a shadow of the man I was. You ask who am I. I wish I knew. I wish I could tell you about the pride and character I once had. My present has tarnished my past and clouded my future. I am an adult man, a good man, a man who has lost his way. You ask who am I. I wish I knew."

Greetings. "I'm known by my name, Bhanu, but that's not me, that's just a tag. My gender, place of birth, nationality, age, marital status, residence, education, titles and employment are simply bits of biographical data. They are signs at a flea market – they attract attention without providing any insight about the merchandise. If you want to know who I am, come walk with me, come talk with me, hold my hand and look into my eyes. Feel my pain and enjoy my smile. Let's break bread together and sip some wine. In that way, you'll discover parts of who I am in ways that are real, not narrative. Who I am is not fully known to me. Each day reveals more, which means, whatever I share today, only describes who I was yesterday."

There are no templates or standard responses to the question: "Who am I?" There are powerful interest groups across the globe, who regard themselves as the custodians of who you and I should be. Keeping account of their views is important. Equally, if not more important, is discovering and unlocking our uniqueness. We are not merely images of invisible, self-appointed sculptors.

> **Someone** *was taking a walk in the park when* **Someone else** *stopped her and said: "Excuse me, can I ask you some questions?"*
> **Someone** *hesitated but then agreed. "Well, first of all," said* **Someone else**, *"who are you?"*
> *"Aah," responded* **Someone**, *"you ask the most difficult questions first."*
> ALAN FLETCHER, THE ART OF LOOKING SIDEWAYS,
> p491
>
> *"...a child is made known to itself by its name."*
> KAREN BLIXEN, AUTHOR: OUT OF AFRICA

Our response to the question "Who am I?" is important. In some way, we reveal our identity, and level of personal ownership. The answers are dynamic as we continue to develop, adapt and evolve through the various phases of our life. We are, and certainly should be work in progress to the very end.

Our reality – who we are, our chosen identity, our persona, is our conversation with the never-ending evolution of life. Whatever character, generosity and creative spirit we are able to achieve, is not solely within our powers of choice. They emerge from honest conversations in our relationship with the larger world in which we live and work.

The ebbs and flows we experience will inevitably affect our well-being – psychological, emotional, spiritual, physical and financial. Those are part of the hard facts of life. Those flows are not mandates to take on new identities. A distinguishing feature of a courageous human being is the ability to retain their identity despite all the pressures to be like everybody else.

Who we are also reveals our leadership. Who we are influences others, just as who they are influences us. Through identity, we lead and are led. Who you are matters. It matters a great deal.

Is 'I' a Fixed Point? Who's to Tell?

Who we are is a tricky business. Human cells are constantly renewing. The latest versions are not the same as they were 15 years ago, which makes them considerably younger than we actually are. "Mirror, Mirror on the wall, who's the fairest of them all?" This famous question by the Wicked Queen, from the story of Snow White and the Seven Dwarfs, seeks only one answer: She is the fairest. But that's an illusion – a fantasy. Only the naïve and ill-informed cling to notions of permanence in all that is human – all that is you, I and us.

Ignorance can be forgiven. Stupidity in the face of hard verifiable evidence, cannot. A collage of photographs taken five years apart, from our personal albums will tell the story. Our diet, circle of colleagues, family, and friends tell many others. Who we are is a celebration of the evolving person we can yet become. Chance will play its part. For the rest, we can explore the pathways that will allow our emerging 'I' to reveal itself to the world. Who 'I' am is not fixed whether we like it or not. Who we were is a matter of memory, record and interpretation. Who we may yet become is the new reimagining horizon our Personal Mastery enables.

How incredibly exciting!

Actions to Develop Your Personal Mastery

Issues that may require your attention	Recommended response to which you should add your own
Eliminate/reduce the flaws in your mindset structures.	Be more discerning about what you accept at face value; Routinely practice Mindset Modelling.
Recognise and correct inconsistencies between what you believe and want to do, and what you actually do.	Improve self-awareness; Invite feedback; Use 360^0 assessments; Be true to your life choices.
Nurture the skills, and courage to correct the flaws, and close, if not completely eliminate the gaps.	Remain open to feedback; Prioritise with consistent practice; Celebrate self-corrections.
Develop the behaviours, skills, values, routines, habits, attitudes, and well-being needed to deliver on your choices; Discard stuff that has passed its shelf-life.	Develop a framework for your personal competences; Prioritise and develop them selectively; Update them periodically; Use the Personal Modelling process steps.
Maintain a great sense of life, love, joy and playfulness as the energisers of your Personal Mastery – lest it becomes a series of heavy tedious tasks, which it most definitely is not.	Look, laugh and live; Recreation; Treasure family and friendships; Practice visitation. Get quality sleep. Enjoy sunsets and sunrises, flowers and seasons. Stay in touch with your dreams.

IN SUMMARY: POINTS TO PONDER

1.
The challenges associated with changing mindsets, behaviours, habits and routines are grossly over-stated.

2.
The biggest blockage is poor awareness and ownership of the opportunities that ongoing renewal and growth offer.

3.
The absence of personal pride and belief in self, coupled with laziness, are major constraints to personal growth.

4.
Eliminating these not so obvious mental constraints is one of the liberating benefits of Personal Mastery in leadership and self-development.

5.
Competence in Personal Mastery serves as an integrating tool – not a prescription – for life and leading.

6.
Happiness, empathy, aspiration, and openness are attitudinal choices. Making them is free.

7.
Values/principles are powerful structures that (should) drive positive human behaviour. Questionable values and gaps between subscription and practice are becoming a serious global problem.

8.
There are no agreed competence standards for leading and leadership.

What would your list include?

WAYPOINT 2: A CALL TO ACTION

The consolidation, reinforcement, and application of learning is personal. Experienced leaders who have used this book as a checklist may have a few pencilled notes on changes they want to make. Other readers may have underlined large sections, added Post-it notes, and opened conversations with colleagues as a part of their approach to application which of course is where the real value of this book lies.

Irrespective of how you intend to proceed, being systematic will add value. Doing so creates structure for your actions, and you know what structure does. An approach I have found useful over the years is to consolidate insights from learning and intended actions into a Learning Log or if you prefer, a Life Journal or Life Book.

There is tremendous value in following a holistic approach when reflecting on how you can, and do have an impact as a leader no matter your age or context. Leading effectively starts with self, and the joy of gathering – effectively growing personally-as a precursor to sharing.

You may already have a Life Journal or working record of your important life choices. Alternatively, you may want to start afresh. A draft template is set out on the next page as a thought-provoker.

Cover page:	Contents:
Title *Your name* *Date last revision*	1. *Purpose of this journal* 2. *Life manifesto* 3. *Core values* 4. *Most important beliefs* 5. *Competence framework* 6. *Career aspirations* 7. *Key routines and habits* 8. *Development priorities* 9. *Dislikes and avoids* 10. *Insights from experience* 11. *Who am I* 12. *Significant things yet to do*
Sections 1-12: *Bulleted text with pictures, photos, drawings, scribblings and sketches*	**Rear cover:** *Inspiring photo/picture* *A few favourite quotations*

This is a super-fun project. It's liberating, invigorating, inspiring and challenging. Are you up to it?

LEADERSHIP WORK

The distinctions between leading and leadership were explained earlier. You will recall that leading occurs irrespective of whether there is intent or not. What we do, and our presence or absence – essentially all our actions – have some impact on the people in our circle of influence. Paradoxically, no action is also an action. As much as our conduct can influence others, so does their conduct influence us.

Leadership is a distinct step up from mere influence. There is intent with action. The action requires purposeful work – tasks, which can be grouped into six primary roles.

- **Awareness**: being in touch with our context, and situations.
- **Responding**: knowing when and how to respond.
- **Resourcing**: securing the resources required for effective action.
- **Partnering**: creating conditions, and relationships that bring out the best in people.
- **Delivery**: getting the job done, and your people safely home – On Brief, On Budget, On Time (OB^{2}T), as coined by Geoff Garrett.
- **Learning**: harvesting experience for continuous improvement.

The roles are an overlay to formally defined leadership responsibilities (tasks) a person may hold – e.g. head of organisation, task group leader, section leader and supervisor. They apply equally to individuals who recognise and accept the importance of leading even though they may not have any formal appointment to do so.

Competences equip people to lead. Authority provides the power to influence. Executing the roles is what gets the leading and leadership job done.

Diagram 19: The six primary leadership roles

Awareness

Learning　　　　　　　　　**Responding**

Delivery　　　　　　　　　**Resourcing**

Partnering

The roles are not completed in sequence nor as a process. They are simultaneous, overlapping, and separate. There is a logic with symmetry. Engaging with them can be orderly, and at times chaotic. Internalising the six roles and mastering the many approaches you can use to fulfil them, blended with your Personal Mastery, provides the foundations for leadership that is relevant, and impactful.

AWARENESS

The underlying principle: Awareness with a reliable understanding of the larger context in which we live and work, and the situations which require our attention, is a prerequisite for effective leadership.

In his *New York Times* best-selling book, Ray Dalio rated as one of the great investors and entrepreneurs of our time, and founder of Bridgewater Associates, a leading private company in the USA, states: "There is nothing more important than understanding how reality works and how to deal with it. The state of mind you bring to this process makes all the difference."

No matter how well we respond to our context, it will be flawed where our perceptions and understanding of the context are flawed. Any failure to respond to a life-threatening situation can be fatal where the threat goes unnoticed. Conversely, to initiate responses to non-existent threats is counter-productive.

Awareness requires active monitoring of those factors in our 'external world' that can significantly impact our context. Such variables as the status and trends in technologies, education, society, trade, digital disruption, industries, health, politics, safety and security, markets, commodities, people, organisations, the economy and demographics matter.

The implications and imperatives of shifts in the technological and innovation landscape are universal, reaching everyone whether we recognise it or not. The number of internet-connected devices and sensors already exceeds 50 billion. The number of mobile cellular subscriptions exceeds 7 billion globally – more than 1 for every person on Earth.

We live in a world of ubiquitous sensing, and connectivity where new methods of artificial intelligence and smart algorithms are continuously adapting and self-correcting. Tens of millions of devices or individuals or teams are simultaneously sharing, and competing thereby creating entirely new architectures for every conceivable industry, and enterprise.

The pattern is clear: Large datasets are describing reality with fine granularity. Google aims to organise all the world's data. Military planners want 'total battlespace awareness'. Leaders at every level need to be in touch with granular information relevant to their situation or risk being swept away by it.

The same need for awareness applies perhaps with lesser urgency and pressure but no less importance, to those leading without formal mandates. Awareness keeps us in touch with the 'here and now and emerging trends'. We can calibrate our perceptions of reality with our understanding of norms and expectations. We are alert to what's happening within and around us and the possible implications thereof. We don't live in a vacuum. We interact with our environment based on our perceptions thereof.

Awareness is not achieved without conscious effort as though we will just somehow 'be aware'. Contextual blindness is a condition associated with autism. Vermeulen defines the condition as 'a reduced spontaneous use of context when giving meaning to a stimulus'. There is a disconnect with reality. Although strongly linked to autism, and not adults at large, the term 'contextual blindness' carries related implications for leaders.

In a mode of 'contextual blindness', people lack the ability to extract relevant meaning from the information they receive about self and their broader context. Despite having the mechanisms and instruments to test and connect the many pieces of reality, disconnected leaders choose to ignore them, and/or craft their own preferred interpretations.

They develop false narratives that will generate flawed decisions and actions. The added and greater risk is that these illusionary states become so embedded the holders can no longer distinguish between reality, and their fictional version of reality. They set the wheels in motion for vicious cycles of self-destruction.

We are fortunate, some may suggest unfortunate, to live in an age of mega information. It comes raw, curated, invited, uninvited and editorially clipped to match our biases and preferences, in multiple formats and from both reputable and malicious sources. Staying abreast of what's happening in the world has never been easier or harder.

More than 20 million Americans still believe the 2020 Presidential Election was 'stolen' despite the complete absence of any proof, over eighty court case rulings against the claim, and several indictments against the ongoing purveyors of the lies. This tragic state of affairs is the opposite of what it means to be aware.

Apart from verifiable scientific facts, descriptions and interpretations of so-called objective reality are always personal, and hence subject to biases. Overcoming or at least minimising this risk is one of the benefits of the mindset modelling process in personal mastery.

Leaders who achieve high impact establish routines such as personal daily updates, regular briefings, and longer-term reviews. Diversity and interactions are important. Valuable sources of information include:

- News resources and reports: daily, weekly and monthly, including from sources that offer information, which is not necessarily aligned with your worldview
- Specialised reports such as peer-reviewed science publications
- Books, magazines and podcasts
- Open-minded, questioning individuals and communities
- Public debates between thought leaders
- Presentations and talks by credible people
- Participation in diverse interest groups
- Personal observation and introspection
- Performance data
- Feedback from credible sources
- Diversity of sources and interactions
- Surveys and the use of analytic tools.

Please don't just read the list. Revise or set up your own. Sharpen and refine it with time. What are the truly important things with which you should keep abreast?

Analytical Tools

There are many tools, techniques and resources available when a more rigorous, and exhaustive analysis of context is required. Their use is a standard routine in planning processes, especially those of a strategic nature. Which tools and who to involve depends on the anticipated implications of the process, resource availability, and time.

Large-scale analysis is frequently undertaken on behalf of major organisations by consulting firms such as Accenture, Deloitte, McKinsey, Roland Berger, and Capgemini. The CIA, the Pentagon, MI5, Mossad, KGB and MSS are intelligence agencies with wide networks of information gathering, analysis, and reporting to keep their respective heads of state in touch with contextual issues, and situations affecting their countries.

These organisations distil and often model the scope and complexity of staying in touch, into curated, cohesive, digestible reports upon which important decisions can be made. The scale of this work may be well beyond what you and I need to lead effectively, but it does serve to highlight the criticality of staying in touch. Irrespective of the route we follow, rigorous testing of perspectives, insights, and conclusions is always important. Useful steps include:

- **Data collection:** What are the facts – wide, and deep?

- **Analysis:** What can be honestly concluded – what is the truth?

- **Prioritisation:** What are the most important needs and opportunities – based on hard facts, and rigorous analysis, not just wishful thinking?

- **Risk assessment:** What are the implications of our take on the realities of our contexts and situations? Sufis – those lovely wise men of the East, teach their students to observe the small signals, hear what is not spoken, and read what is not written. Awareness requires sensing beyond the obvious.

Diagrams 20 and 21 provide examples of how we can map the information we want to collect. Set up your routines, make a list of what you need for reliable awareness, and do it now.

Diagram 20: Macro Contextual Analysis: Checklist

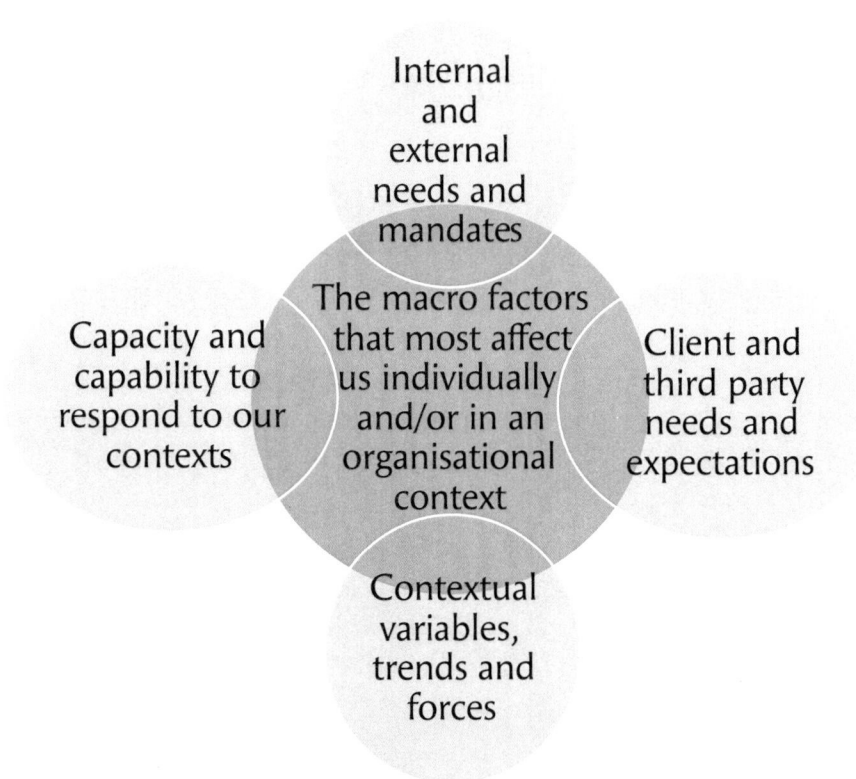

Internal and external needs and mandates

The macro factors that most affect us individually and/or in an organisational context

Capacity and capability to respond to our contexts

Client and third party needs and expectations

Contextual variables, trends and forces

Awareness

Diagram 21: Analysis of Influencing Forces: Checklist

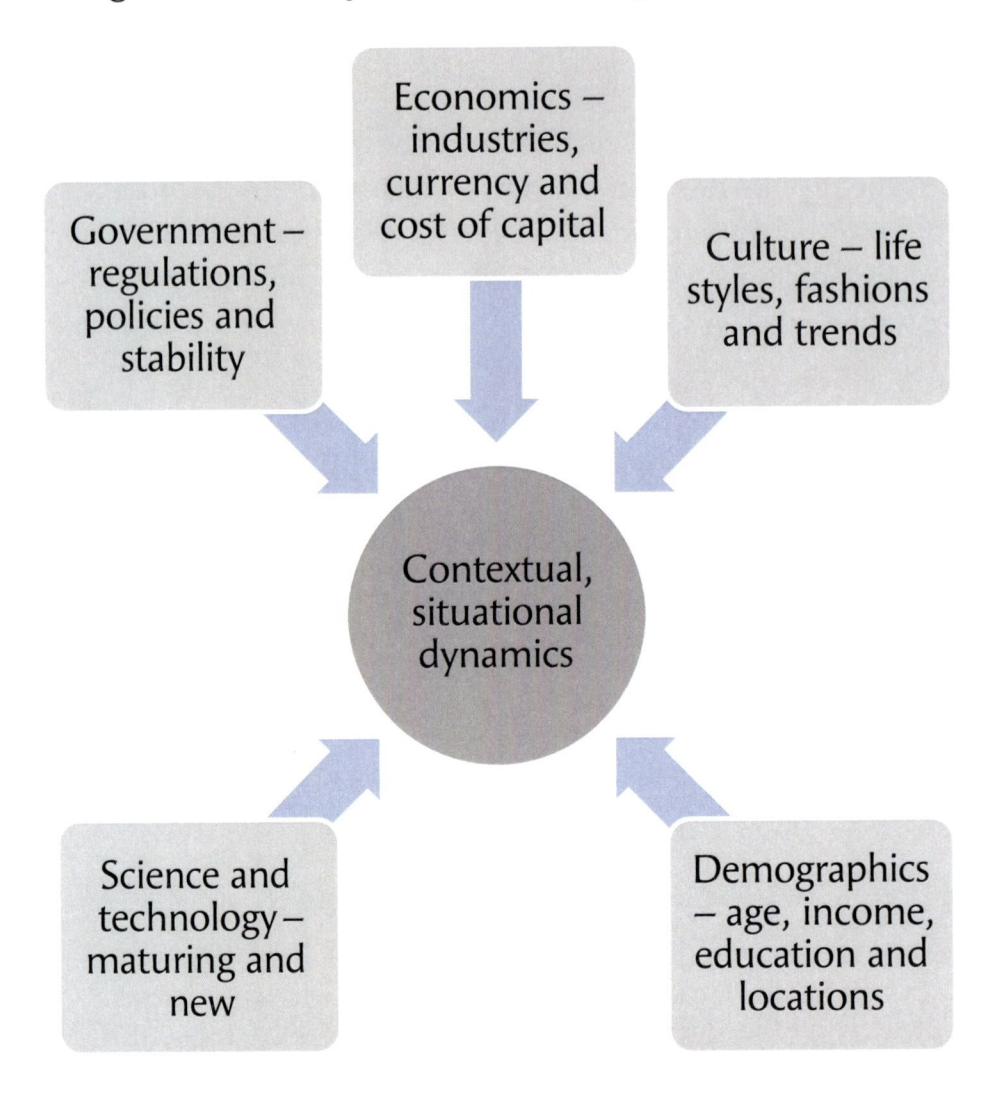

- Government – regulations, policies and stability
- Economics – industries, currency and cost of capital
- Culture – life styles, fashions and trends
- Science and technology – maturing and new
- Demographics – age, income, education and locations

→ Contextual, situational dynamics

"All great truths are obvious truths. But not all obvious truths are great truths."
— ALDOUS HUXLEY

RESPONSES

Classic literature and teaching on leadership narrowly define determining strategy and direction as the primary responsibility of leaders. That is limited and frankly wrong.

People are trapped in a building that is burning out of control. A fellow student is being physically molested by a belligerent teacher. Your executive team is in open rebellion against the plans you have just submitted to the Board of Directors. Your teachers are refusing to implement a new syllabus. Your child has not returned home as arranged from a social event.

Urgent action is required. How do you respond?

Well, whatever our response is, it's not going to include thoughts about determining strategic direction. There are zillions of issues, problems and opportunities people have to deal with on a daily basis, none of which have anything to do with strategy.

Our instinctive responses depend on:

- Awareness – do we actually recognise situations or events that require action; none so blind as those who will not see?

- The urgency and importance of action that may be required.

- Our competence to deal with the situation.

- Our power base.

- What resources are available?

- Our common sense and adaptability.

Does the situation call for immediate action, or can it be deferred, and if so, until when? Urgency and importance may be nano-second computations upon which we must act.

> **Leadership is the actions taken to achieve results through the efforts of other people.**

The Holy Grail of Leadership
(Oxford: Holy Grail – something that you want very much but that is very hard to get or achieve.)

As important as they may be, every action we take in the process of leading can be regarded as a preamble, a foreplay to the point at which leadership kicks in.

Leadership comes to life when we '**step up, and assert influence**'. The action may be inadequate but that beats not responding when leadership is necessary.

Leaders are not passive observers. **Stepping up** is the Holy Grail of leadership. The steps recommended in Diagram 22 are the very least that 'stepping up' entails.

Diagram 22: Stepping up: The Holy Grail of Leadership

Action	Activation
1. Get attention	You have to assert your presence in some appropriate manner. Raise your voice. Shout if necessary. Stand up. Jump up. Interrupt whatever is happening. Be silent. Glare. Stare. Submit a report. Call people to attention. Find the decision-makers who can initiate change. Speak to them. You are completely wasting your time if you are not heard.
2. Clarify the situation	Briefly describe your take on the situation. What is happening? You may need to test your perception(s) with those present as a reality check. This assumes you have time for this action, and that what is happening may not be obvious to others.
3. Outline outcomes	Briefly describe the desired outcome(s) – if you can. It is unrealistic to think leaders will always have solutions or where they do, the best solutions. Assuming time is available, get people involved in each of the steps 2 to 6.
4. Clarify process options	Briefly state the process steps to achieve the outcome(s). If time, encourage participation.
5. Clarify responsibilities	Clarify what needs to be done by whom, and by when.
6. Get commitment for action	Ideally ensure that you get the understanding, and acceptance of the people involved. In certain instances where you have positional authority, you may need to order compliance.

These six steps with appropriate tweaks for situational issues represent '**leadership in action**'. Following them will equip you to deal with events requiring spontaneous leadership response(s), and those where more time is available.

In an ideal world, your voice tone may be warm, accommodating as you '**step up**' to get attention. In an emergency, you may be direct, rapid and devoid of niceties. On one occasion, during a planning meeting, a senior manager unexpectedly jumped up, and shouted out "I've had enough of this team, and all the BS we have to put up with from our director – I'm leaving." I jumped up, ran to the door and blocked his exit while demanding that he calms down and returns to his seat. Was that '**leadership in action**' or not?

Yes, it was, and he did stay on to make a valuable contribution. Striving for career advancement is a different way of getting attention. Purchasing flowers for a loved one, inviting staff to morning refreshments in your office, publicly thanking people – junior/senior and even strangers to you – for their contributions, and reaching out to support people are a few of the many, many ways we can '**step up**'.

Older readers will recall the popular TV series *MacGyver*, which followed the adventures of Angus MacGyver, a secret agent equipped with extensive scientific resourcefulness to solve problems using any combination of materials at hand. He tackled many seemingly unsolvable problems armed only with duct tape and his Swiss Army knife.

Life is not a TV show. We all have considerably more than duct tape and a pocket knife with which to deal with diverse problems and opportunities.

Different situations may need, and allow for short, and/or medium, and/or long, and/or ongoing responses. Multiple planning tools and techniques are available when deeper analysis, and evaluation are justified. The basics include a systematic approach to problem-solving, and the ability to prepare an action plan. Diagrams 23 and 24 provide examples of these bread-and-butter skills.

Diagram 23: 6-Step problem-solving technique

1. Identify and describe the apparent problem/opportunity.

2. Collect information, separating facts from assumptions and inferences.

3. Define the real problem(s) (normally as a question), e.g. "How to .... so that ...."

4. Generate possible solutions/courses of action.

5. Evaluate the merits/risk/potential/implications of respective options.

6. Select the best (perfect versus fit for purpose versus affordable versus minimum requirement) and develop a suitable plan for implementation.

Diagram 24: Sample action plan

Action Plan Title: Vision Development

Objective: To develop and implement a vision for ABC Department so that research staff have a long term perspective within which to plan short to medium term work.

(Statement of intended action (future tense))

(Statement of desired outcome)

Performance standards:
(This plan will have been met when)

(e-SMART metrics (present tense))

a. **Staff participation:** All staff in ABC ... participate in the initiative to develop and implement a vision for the Dept. At least 75% actively make a contribution via debate and discusssion which leads to the formulation, acceptance and implementation of the vision.

b. **Rigour:** The initiative is rigorous and special attention is paid to exploring and considering a wide range of options with an in-depth analysis of the consequences pertaining to the most promising. Staff confirm that diverse thought and ideas are encouraged prior to final selection.

c. **Understanding and acceptance (buy-in):** The HoD and other senior leaders ensure that all ABC staff understand whatever vision is finally selected. Feedback from staff confirms that at least 85% are fully engaged for implementation and achievement.

d. **Implementation plan and milestones:** A plan with clear milestones and accountabilities is prepared to achieve the vision. In particular, the part key role-players in ABC must play in this regard, is defined in writing.

e. **Timing:** The vision is developed and implementation starts by no later than *Insert Date*.

Accountability:
Overall accountability for the successful execution of this action plan resides with *Insert Name*

Example of an action plan

Action Step	Complete by Date	Accounta-bility	Time Budget	Status
1. Prepare a 'briefing' document on vision and set an assignment for ABC staff to identify the key elements they would like included in the Department's vision. Forward briefing to HoD (or director) for final editing and approval.	Day-month	You	2.5 hrs	

Action Step	Complete by Date	Accounta-bility	Time Budget	Status
2. Sign off on Briefing document (with or without amendments).	Day-month	HoD	.5 hr	
3. Select working groups of approximately 12 to 15 each, covering all departmental staff. Circulate Briefing document and request that staff diarise the feedback meetings as scheduled in the document.	Day-month	You	1 hr	
4. Working groups meet (round 1) to complete an assignment on vision. Post first/early responses on notice boards/websites for all groups to see.	Day-month	Group Leaders	2 hrs	
5. Groups collect information from each other (directly and/or from notice boards/websites) and meet (round 2) to fine-tune their perspectives and formulate first draft visions, which are again posted for the other groups to see	Day-month	Group Leaders	2 hrs	
6. HoD and senior leaders meet to formulate a response to the first 'draft' formulations and provide commentary/feedback to the groups. Also, discuss with Director.	Day-month	HoD	3 hrs	

Action Step	Complete by Date	Accounta-bility	Time Budget	Status
7. Groups collect information from each other (directly and/or from notice boards/websites) and meet (round 3) to fine-tune their 'ideal' vision and prepare a short presentation for a large group plenary.	Day-month	Group Leaders	1 hr	
8. HoD and Snr leaders meet to review current thinking and expectations.	Day-month	HoD	2 hrs	
9. Staff attend a plenary session during which working groups present their 'ideal' visions for the Department with a short commentary on expected implications. Groups have chances to discuss, deliberate and fine-tune a 'first choice' vision for the Dept. Implications are discussed. Early milestones and measures are identified. Staff are requested to reflect on the vision and the parts that they each will need to play in order to ensure that it is achieved.	Day-month	Group Leaders	4.5 hrs	
10. HoD presents vision, measures and milestones to staff during plenary sessions. Acceptance for the vision is tested together with clarity on the process for implementation and achievement.	Day-month	HoD	3 hrs	

Action Step	Complete by Date	Accountability	Time Budget	Status
11. Communication plan to report on progress, reinforce focus and retain open lines of interaction is implemented to maintain momentum	Day-month	As assigned by HoD	Ongoing	

AP Originator: HoD   Date:

Final Accountability: HoD   Planned completion:

Sound planning is an important part of how leaders respond. The permutations, and variations in planning formats are endless ranging from simple to extremely complex plans – electronically compiled on sophisticated templates catering for hundreds/thousands of people, product developments, launch plans, defensive, and attacking strategies to 10-year economic growth plans.

Being involved in the formulation of plans of this nature does not in itself constitute leading, and leadership. It demonstrates planning skills. The leadership resides in recognising the need for detailed planning – awareness – **'stepping up'** to get them prepared, accepted, resourced, effectively implemented – OB^2T, and successfully delivered.

Pre-emptive or contingency action based on anticipation is the high end of a leader's response role. Anticipating problems, and opportunities before they appear, requires a much higher level of awareness and appreciation of the implications. This includes anticipating the unintended consequences of well-intended responses.

> *It always pays to get your retaliation in first.*
> – WILLIE JOHN MCBRIDE, FAMOUS BRITISH LIONS RUGBY PLAYER.

Responses

Having observed the need-awareness, an anticipatory response is exemplified by the person who passes the salt at the dinner table before it is requested.

The leadership responses by the senior decision-makers in Amazon have been well ahead of their time. With awareness of emerging digital technologies, leaders in Amazon pre-emptively built a global network of over 80 fulfilment centres, and they keep broadening their product range with delivery that can match the best main street retailers.

Decision Criteria for Response Selection

Fortunately, the majority of the responses generated by leaders do not require exhaustive analysis. Where justified on the basis of risk, and possible implications, major responses should be subjected to pre-implementation evaluation based on relevant criteria.

Here are a few that may be considered. Are we:

- Responding to valid contextual needs, opportunities, tested assumptions and beliefs?

- Considering responses that are consistent with our principles and life choices?

- Focussing (concentrating) our critical resources on the most important needs and opportunities?

- Avoiding the senseless carrying over of outdated structures, processes and projects?

- Using SMART metrics for our proposed actions – stretching, measurable, achievable, realistic, and time-linked?

- Leveraging our strengths?

RESOURCING

The Southern Party on board the "Nimrod." Left to right: Wild, Shackleton, Marshall, Adams

MEN WANTED for hazardous journey, small wages, bitter cold, long months of complete darkness, constant danger, safe return doubtful, honor and recognition in case of success.
Ernest Shackleton 4 Burlington st.

The 'Men Wanted' ad tells a story of bias and the higher appeal of recognition above money. Money and means are important resources. Never more so than the fabric of people. People without money and means can at least make a plan. Money and means without people are artefacts. That may change with AI, greater automation, and new discoveries in the years ahead. For now and the foreseeable future, competent people remain a leader's **number one resource**.

One bad apple in a team can completely compromise the collective brilliance of all the players. The top coaches and organisational leaders know this only too well. When one person becomes a legend in their own mind and heaven forbid that person is the captain, head chef, top litigator or CEO, sub-standard performance will be the order of the day.

Attracting the right people, and optimising the selection process are therefore critical tasks. Google follows a six-step process, and Apple has three. They are well documented on the web. Sports teams look for track record, age, and assessed potential. I start with attitude. Apart from initial screening, and verifications which can be undertaken by support staff, leaders should have the final decision regarding who gets to be on their team. Organisational routines that assign people to a team or unit, without the final approval of the accountable leader, may be necessary but will always be a sub-optimal practice.

Four Resourcing Routines

When resourcing for people, there are four minimum principles to apply whether you are making the final appointment decision, inheriting team members or seeking voluntary collaboration from people for whom you have no stewardship responsibility. They are:

- Only **select on merit** even if that requires delaying the appointment. Absolutely only on merit.

- Never select without requiring a **demonstration** – ideally several, of the competences you expect the person to have, and which they claim to have.

- Never select without **stress testing** the person's ability to handle unexpected, and even confrontational situations – not as an explanation of what they would do – but by actually dealing with the situation/scenarios you create.

- **Test** their **self-insight** by concluding each interview by asking them to provide – verbally – a self-evaluation of how they believe they performed during the interaction. Ask at any stage, what the significant things/projects they still want to complete for an indication of their aspirations. For more senior-level individuals, add a request for them to share significant learning/experiences over the past two to three years and how they have used them.

The same process can be followed with existing team members you inherit in order to form a first-hand impression of what they bring to the team. The manner in which this is undertaken must be positioned with sensitivity and respect.

Any person, no matter how competent, is going to struggle to meet delivery expectations without the tools and equipment needed for the job. Securing those resources is a leadership responsibility. Operating budgets, plant, equipment, materials, facilities, support structures and some level of assuredness about continuity, are all items for consideration. The possibilities are endless.

Organisations with the best people win more consistently than others. Find the best. Recruit the best. Challenge the best to be better. Nurture those who have the aspiration, and matching potential to be part of the best. Never lose sight of the fact that having the best is no substitute for how well the parts work together.

PARTNERING

For centuries, conventional wisdom and research have ingrained the belief that leaders motivate and inspire people by providing inter alia:

- Incentives, rewards and recognition.
- Opportunities for growth and achievement.
- Safety and security.
- Captivating speeches and alluring visions.
- Discipline and reprimand. Power and independence.

There is validity in these beliefs from a historical perspective. Leaders could and can still ignite emotions, sway minds and provoke action when interacting with vulnerable, unsuspecting people. People who suffer the plight of illiteracy, limited education, closed social networks, dominant religions, and political dogmas. Dependent people who are relatively easy to exploit.

The flawed canvas of charismatic leaders who are saviours of the world – champions of our safety and well-being – is universally reinforced in popular media. There is still an insatiable appetite for the prince charming lover, the divine saviour, billionaire boffin and fictional reincarnation of the ideal self.

While they certainly still apply, these age-old beliefs are expedient and flawed. They ignore the very essence of what motivation is and means. Leaders with integrity and respect for others do not assume or take any rights for the motivation of others. On the contrary, contemporary leaders have an entirely different approach to the work of motivating others.

Motivation is a state of mind – one which causes an individual to be positively disposed towards something thereby inducing energy and attraction. Conversely, the state of mind may be negative or indifferent, thereby inducing dislike and avoidance. That state of mind belongs exclusively to the owner of the mind. Every person must always, and under all circumstances recognise their right and responsibility to motivate themselves.

It is not my responsibility to motivate you nor yours to motivate me. How dare others, and in this case, leaders take that right away from each of us. What does that do for you and me? Are we and others expected to sit around and wait for some hero to arrive on their white horse, and motivate us?

What utter, utter and complete BS. When parents, folks in education and leaders in all walks of life eliminate the outdated altruistic belief that they must motivate others, the impact of their influence changes dramatically – for the better. There is a fine and subtle difference between contributing to the motivation of others, and assuming your actions switch their state of mind.

Offer any inducement you like. "Carol, here's a million for you to complete the outstanding assignment." Who has the final say on whether they will complete the assignment or not? "Sam, if you do not change your attitude, we are going to dismiss you." Who is in charge of that attitude?

By offering support, encouragement and even threats, leaders can and do influence 'states of mind' but they never own them. After all, who motivates the motivator? Who motivates the CEO, the director general, the president and anybody else you care to mention?

They do. And we do.

The actions taken to influence the state of mind of others – to supposedly motivate them – is a joint venture between people, between leaders and those they are seeking to lead. When a scholar stands up in a forum and spontaneously thanks a teacher for their dedicated approach to learning, can that have an influence on the teacher's state of mind? Definitely. What that influence entails depends on whether the teacher experiences the comments as praise or veiled cynicism. The teacher is the final arbiter of her mind.

In sports, coaches are often treated like 'gods'. The best are assumed to have amazing powers of motivation. They certainly do have considerable influence until they discover their inducements no longer lift sagging performance and morale. 'The coach has lost the dressing room' is the common excuse.

British Football is a graveyard for renowned coaches who have fallen in love with their fabled powers of motivation. Those who survive, coaches like Sir Alex Ferguson, Arsene Wenger, Pep Guardiola, and their counterparts in all sports across the globe, have learnt that they are in a partnership with the players. As much as they can inspire and influence their players, the players inspire, and influence them with each retaining the right to decide how that influence affects them.

"You make me so unhappy." Hello, wake up.

Nobody can make you unhappy without your permission. Effective leaders never surrender that permission nor do they take it from others.

The role of partnering in leadership extends to all activities. Short-term crisis situations requiring leadership intervention may prevent the building of a longer-term 'partnering relationships'. That should be the exception not the norm.

An attitude of partnering creates a collaborative win-win culture where all the parties strive to achieve their goals while assisting others to achieve theirs. They build common ground and value the benefits of mutual success. The well-being of the members of labour unions depends on the success, and survival of the employers. The employers have a similar dependence on the unions.

Adversarial relationships in business, government, institutions, communities, and between people, destroy value and trigger outcomes that nobody in their right mind wants. Competent leaders who pursue a partnering approach, do not intentionally act in ways that are counter-productive to human values. They strive to build, improve, and uplift, not hurt, or destroy.

In an earlier life, I worked as an instructor at a military institution training career officers. The model followed was much the same as that used by similar organisations around the world. Upon arrival, the cadets were randomly allocated to one of six platoons. Each platoon had an instructor who was responsible for their leadership and physical and academic training for a three-month period. The cadets were continuously evaluated, and platoon performances were monitored.

After three months, the platoons remained the same while the instructors were rotated to serve as new role models and objective assessors. In my final rotation, I was allocated a platoon that had, seen holistically performed poorly during the previous three months. This was not an assignment I welcomed as my earlier platoons had consistently ranked in the top one or two. At the first meeting upon taking charge, I read the riot act to these cadets informing them that I planned to double their workload, and pressure until they started performing to my expectations. Over the next four weeks, their performance to my immense frustration continued to decline. Where was I failing as their leader?

The pain and humiliation were excruciating when my chief instructor flagged a lesson I knew so well but had violated so badly. That crucially important lesson is applicable to all aspects of life not only to leading and leadership.

From the outset, I had made it clear to the platoon members that I had no faith in them. They were a disappointment. Compared to other platoons, they were just a bunch of losers. "But don't worry, I'll fix that. I'll get them back on track," I had proclaimed. How naïve can one be?

Seated in a circle, the correction took the form of an apology and two requests. Firstly, would they be willing to accept the apology keeping in mind that the simple act of apologising does not erase errors? Secondly, could we re-contract – start again – and work together to find ways to ignite the performance they were capable of achieving? I received two affirmatives that day and a proud moment eight weeks later when they completed their program as the runners-up having moved from last to second position.

Same people. Same tasks. Same challenges. Only two variables had changed. The attitude – including approach and behaviour – of the instructor, and the mindset of the cadets. In partnership, a new contract and outcome had been achieved.

Our ability to motivate, and inspire – really to cocreate an environment wherein all players choose to belong and excel is influenced by everything we do as a leader, and equally important, fail to do.

Co-creating Conditions Wherein People Can Excel

The partnering role is a contracting role. A role of relationship building and creating space for people to blossom. Netflix, Patagonia, and Nordstrom have pioneered the move away from performance management to performance contracting. Building adaptive cultures which amplify ownership, and autonomy within shared boundaries is the leading edge of partnering. 'We trust, and believe in you' is the mantra.

The **basics** include recognising and respecting diversity and avoiding prejudice, especially discrimination based on gender, culture, race, sexual preferences, religion and age. Treating people with dignity, and respect irrespective of their station in life. Contracting on mutual performance expectations. Assisting with the provision of resources. Providing and requesting feedback – discussion – on performance, and competence development. Displaying genuine belief in people. Rewarding achievements, and where necessary, applying discipline to address deviations.

There are hundreds of little things leaders can do to live out a partnering relationship. In another earlier life, I attended a short session where the Senior Officer of an operational unit with 40,000 people had invited the cleaning and gardening staff to his office. They were a small group of staff from modest backgrounds. Although employed by a different unit from his, he wanted to meet them personally.

Strolling to the front of his magnificent desk – a symbol some leaders regard as their throne – speaking in a welcoming voice he said: "You know many functions are held at these premises to host senior international dignitaries. On each occasion, I receive many compliments about the beautiful gardens and high standards of cleanliness. I value those comments but must declare the credit belongs to you. You create a positive first impression. You are the people making the difference. Thank you. We stand together with pride. Thank you."

Then he shook each person's hand, holding it for several seconds which felt like an eternity as he maintained eye contact. What many would regard as an everyday courtesy, was for them a huge leap of acknowledgement. They existed. The most senior leader had set time aside for them. He had looked them in the eye. He had held their hand. He had touched their soul.

Interestingly John Wooden who coached the UCLA basketball team to 10 national championships, including seven in a row was more passionate about teaching than championships. One of his little touches was to insist that players are punctual, and neatly dressed before he would allow them on the team.

> *The main ingredient in stardom is the rest of the team.*
> – COACH JOHN WOODEN.

Securing Understanding and Acceptance

Partnering is a fallacy without genuine buy-in – understanding and acceptance – from all the parties involved or affected. Acceptance is the minimum threshold to achieve. It is unrealistic to expect that all parties will always agree with every aspect of desired actions. We can disagree and still accept an action.

In the spirit of partnering, understanding and acceptance (U/A) should never be taken for granted. Securing U/A in organisations can be far ranging including U/A for:

- The strategic intent, vision, mission, and strategic goals of an organisation.
- Ongoing tasks – primary and secondary work.
- Organisational and team values.
- Projects and priorities.
- Budgets, and resource allocations.
- Support staff service level contracts.
- Individual roles and responsibilities.
- Performance improvement projects and initiatives.

- Ad hoc initiatives which are over and above normal expectations.
- Policies, procedures and operating routines.
- Standards of performance and conduct.
- Safe working practices.
- Quality standards.
- Organisation structure and reporting arrangements
- Self-improvement plans.
- Changes and amendments to all of the aforementioned.

The often-quoted colloquial phrase **'It ain't over till the fat lady sings'** is attributed to many sources. It means that the final outcome of an event cannot be predicted until it has come to a conclusion.

The leadership roles of awareness, responses, resourcing and partnering are the **'step up and take charge show'** of leading and leadership. But **'it ain't over until the fat lady sings'** and that outcome occurs with **'delivery'**. Everything that has gone before may be commendable and textbook perfect. It counts for nothing – truly nothing – until delivery has been successfully concluded. **The fat lady must sing.**

DELIVERY

Effort is important. Results count. Sacrifices beyond the call of duty are admirable. Without results, they are in vain. Achieving 95% of a goal is better than achieving anything less. Unfortunately, achieving 95% means the goal was not met unless that variance was factored in at some stage.

Dynamic adjustments of goals and actions may be justified based on circumstances that have changed since implementation commenced. Affected parties should **always be kept informed**, and where necessary, involved in deciding on the changes. Caution should be exercised where nothing less than perfect delivery – on brief, on budget, on time (OB^{2}T) – is expected, and required.

A leader's word is their bond. A commitment is a pledge of honour. Acceptance of responsibilities and all that goes with them creates an obligation. Competent, reliable leaders deliver – OB^{2}T. They are trusted. There are few things in the world that compromise who we are and what we stand for, than breaking our word. "I'll look into it. I'll get back to you on that. I'll attend. Be assured the task will be completed before the weekend. I'll send you the report." Cheap words from people when they fail to pitch up, stand up, and deliver. **The fat lady must sing.**

LEARNING

- If you have two possible trajectories for life, is it more advantageous to select 'no learning required' or 'life-long learning is a non-negotiable imperative'?
- Is it better to detect and correct the error or ignore it?
- Should we wait for government or some form of divine intervention to improve our quality of life or learn our way to where we strive to be?

No learning, no progress. No learning, just stagnation and decay. People have to learn their way out of poverty. The great hand in the sky is not going to reach out no matter how devoted we are. I wish it was otherwise, but pragmatism tells a different tale.

People have to learn their way up the ladder. We have to learn how to survive. We have to learn our way to achievement and recognition. We have to learn our way into loving relationships. None of these outcomes are achieved without learning. How can learning ever be less than a mega imperative for every person on Planet Earth?

That imperative places learning at the forefront of any leader's agenda. If we want to lead – have a positive ethical influence on others, and step up to leadership – achieve results through the efforts of others – we sure as hell need to be deeply versed in the fine art of learning.

At an employment level, individual, team and organisational learning all contribute to building adaptive and competitive capacity. The benefits of doing so speak for themselves.

The learning role in leadership entails:

- Being a strong advocate for learning.

- Setting a personal example for ongoing learning.

- Providing focussed support for learning initiatives.

- Acknowledging and where possible rewarding learning achievement.

At a graduation dinner several years ago, I sat opposite the then-CEO of BHP Billiton, the largest Mining House in the world. For 90 minutes, he discreetly asked one question after another. "Professor, how does the Engineering Faculty decide on course curricula? Dr, what criteria do you use to assess the value of practical assignments? John, which teaching methodologies did you enjoy the most?"

And so it went. After the dinner, I asked him about his approach, and why he had not used the forum to perhaps promote BHP as a desirable career destination for young engineers. "There are other ways of attracting talented staff," he replied. "But the opportunity to tap into the insights and experience of leading academics is an opportunity not to be missed. Never stop asking questions. Never stop learning."

During hundreds of on-site visits to staff on multiple levels, Dr Geoff Garrett, at the time the CEO of a globally acclaimed scientific research organisation, consistently started his conversations with a simple question: "What have you learnt since we last met?" Where time allowed it was followed by a second straightforward question: "How have you applied your learning, and how has that application benefitted you, and our organisation?"

What would you predict was one of the dominant value drivers in that organisation's culture? Parents who consistently pose similar questions to their family and friends send powerful messages about the things that really matter in life.

You know that value has become embedded when you are confronted in a whimsical, and fun manner by family, and friends who pose the questions to you before you get a chance. What would you predict happens beforehand when people know those questions are coming their way?

Contrast that with the youngster who is out walking with his father when a Boeing Dreamliner flies overhead. With excitement, the youngster tugs the father's arm and asks: "Daddy, daddy look at that plane. Several hundred people with all their luggage. Several hundred tons of metal and fuel. How does that plane stay in the air?"

"Great question, son, but I don't know the answer."

They stroll on and approach an extended row of large overhead power lines. "Daddy, daddy," comes the charged voice: "Somewhere to the North, there is a thing called a power station sending electricity along those lines so that at home we can throw a switch to get light from an LED. Gosh, Dad, how does that all work?"

"Another great question son, but I don't exactly know the answer."

"Well, OK then, Dad, at least tell me how those leaves over there clean this invisible air we are breathing. I don't see any dirt or movement in the leaves."

"That's beyond me my boy. I really don't know, but I'm proud of you asking all these questions because that's how you learn."

Really? We learn when we get the answers not just from posing the questions. What are the questions for which you do not have answers? Leaders from parents to great educationalists to role players across the globe, relentlessly and ceaselessly stoke the fire of curiosity and assist with actions that lead towards finding the answers.

> *I was born not knowing and have had only a little time to change that here and there.*
> – RICHARD FEYNMAN, NOBEL LAUREATE

The popular theory of learning developed by psychologist David Kolb provides a useful template to describe how knowledge is created through experience. Kolb's theory explains that concrete experience, reflective observation, abstract conceptualisation and active experimentation form a four-stage process for effective learning as shown in Diagram 25.

The four highlighted words reflect the original Kolb Model. For our Twiddly Bits, I've removed the arrows depicting a sequence between the phases and added a few notations in brackets.

To **experience** we must be willing to explore and accumulate experiences. That is easier said than done when people lack opportunities and are risk-averse. The leader's role in learning is to create opportunities, and provide safe landing spaces for failure. People learn to balance by falling.

Reflecting what you are learning and what it means is essential. Remove that step from the cycle, and much of the value of learning gets lost. This happens regularly because people fail to reflect on what they are learning. The potential benefits of reflection quadruple when undertaken with others. Schools, colleges, organisations, and voluntary groups such as art, reading, music, craft and ecology are a sampling of many communities that arrange exchanges to 'think about' their learning in open forums.

Leaders who keep asking the 'what have you learnt' questions, scholars who self-organise into study groups, and initiatives that promote collective learning are powerful vehicles for **accelerated**

high-quality learning. For those who may not have recently thought about it, learning with application at a rate faster than the norm creates competitive advantages not easily matched.

Learning like leadership and personal mastery is not a sequential process. The messy practice of learning and unlearning, of mastering and failing are the realities of leadership that seeks to help people tease out the best in themselves.

You are either passionate about the contribution you can make to individual, team, community and organisational learning or you are not. The contribution comes from the heart, not a job description or hunger for credits.

Diagram 25: Modified Kolb Cycle of Learning

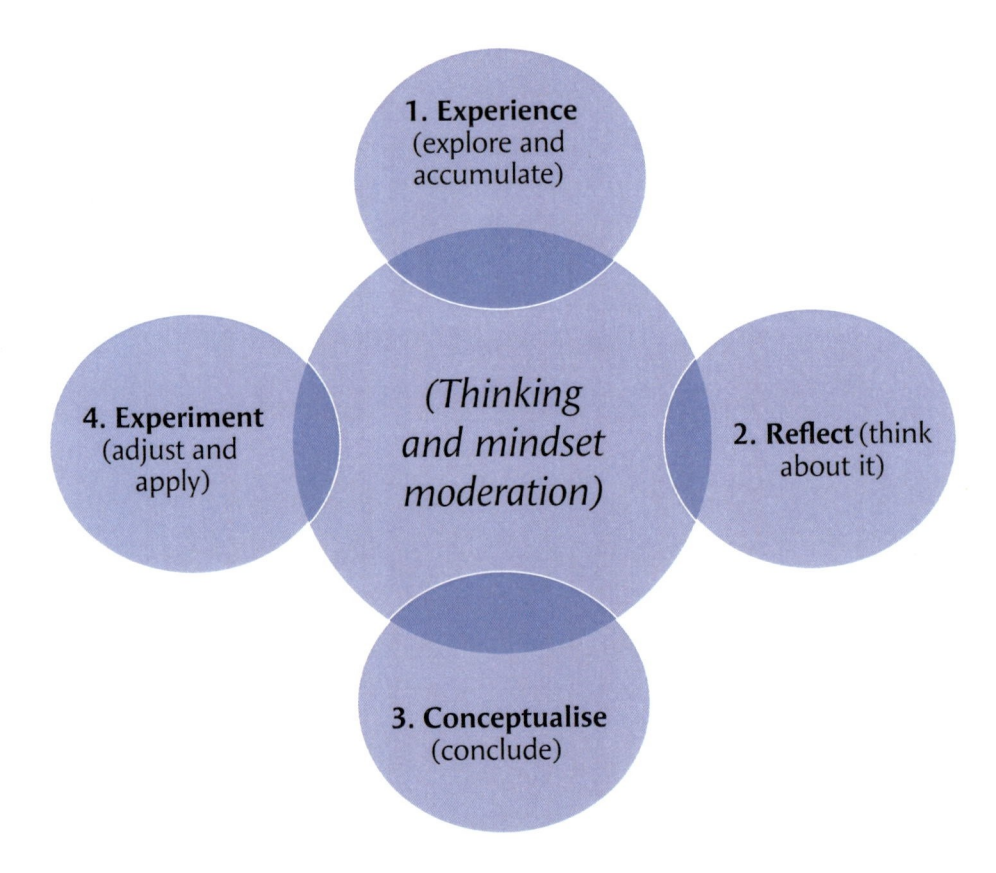

1. **Experience** (explore and accumulate)

2. **Reflect** (think about it)

3. **Conceptualise** (conclude)

4. **Experiment** (adjust and apply)

(Thinking and mindset moderation)

Useful actions leaders can take in the learning space are:

- Do not assume responsibility for another person's learning and development.

- Personally nurture from the earliest moment you can, a love, and passion for learning.

- Encourage everybody from your significant others to the CEO, to have a Personal Development Plan wherein they pragmatically detail their learning needs/objectives and their proposed pathways to finding the answers to the questions they cannot answer. Pragmatic. Specific. No generalisations. No psycho-babble. No hubris. From a leadership perspective, it is frankly immoral to have some form of stewardship responsibility for people and not challenge them about their learning. Spouses and life partners included.

- Confucius reportedly said, "Even the faintest ink is better than the strongest memory." Encourage people to take and keep notes. Be appalled by people who fiddle on their mobiles while attending meetings and lectures. Their learning, value and contribution coefficient is zero.

- Where it is within your power, set up routines for collectives – groups or teams of people with shared interests – to meet, share and capture their learning.

- At an organisational level, establish or at least request that experiences are regularly captured, distilled and shared with those who are open to learning from others. The major global consulting firms and corporates are masterful in this regard. From parents to offspring, craftsperson to apprentice and generation to generation, capturing and distilling relevant experiences builds the wisdom of ages. The benefits of doing so are staggering.

- Be a champion for learning. Acknowledge your errors. Learn from them. Set an example that it's not a crime to fail. What we do with the richness of experiences and learning is what matters most.

Would you delete learning as a leadership role? How effective and satisfied you are in life correlates with your capacity to absorb and apply learnng – your own and that which you can draw from others.

What value does your learning add to others?

IN SUMMARY: POINTS TO PONDER

1.
Leadership roles: awareness, responses, resourcing, partnering, delivery and learning.

2.
The Holy Grail of leadership: Step up and be heard.

3.
Clarify the situation, outcome(s), process, responsibilities and commitment to action.

4.
Dig for causes and real problems.

5.
Big decisions: People in? People out?

6.
It is not a leader's job to motivate people.

7.
Who motivates the leader?

8.
People can't do what they don't understand. What they don't accept, they won't do. There is always a way in. Always. Find it.

9.
The fat lady must sing – deliver OB^2T.

10.
Life without learning is a waste of our greatest asset: The capacity to grow, adapt and unlock our potential.

AT WHAT POINT IS A PERSON COMPETENT TO LEAD?

Do we not all want to know?

To answer this question, we must return to an earlier question: "To what do you attribute your success?" I hope you gave it some thought and enjoyed the responses. It would be hard to build a case for success that did not at least include the following:

- Our competences.

- Consistent, reliable delivery of results, OB^2T.

- Support we have received along the way.

- Luck.

The second bullet provides the ultimate metric for leader success. We can have an exemplary repertoire of competences with abundant support from family, friends, and colleagues. Luck helps but is unpredictable. Without consistently reliable delivery through the efforts of the people we have mobilised – that point at which the fat lady sings – you are looking at means, and effort, not outcome.

The results, and the means used to achieve them, should ideally always be ethical and constructive. The fact that this may not be the case does not cancel the reality of delivery. The notorious Pablo Escobar styled his global drug operations under the guise of social upliftment. He enjoyed wide support despite the condemnation of law enforcement agencies. He mobilised thousands of poppy-growing farmers, drug processing facilities, a global distribution network, a well-armed security infrastructure, and a sophisticated grey money laundering system.

Was he effective with high impact as a leader? For sure. He delivered significant results through the efforts of a vast network of people. Was he ethical and would you follow him are entirely different matters.

When we look at our own leadership, and that of others, we may reasonably think that the evidence of consistent delivery – OB^2T – indicates competence. At one level, it does, and that cannot be refuted. That perception unfortunately draws people into making flawed conclusions. Delivery alone is only part of the story.

Millions of people have over centuries followed rogue leaders. Twenty-plus million people still follow Donald Trump despite his litany of lies, bullying and violations of constitutional obligations. The fact that he is a high achiever says nothing about what he is achieving and the methods he applies.

Technically a person is competent to lead when:

- They are able to consistently mobilise the efforts of others to achieve results, typically results they would not have pursued, and achieved without the leader's intervention.

- The results achieved are relevant and have an impact.

- They do so in an ethical and sustainable manner.

- People are not exploited, abused or manipulated.

That is the cold hard reality of leading and leadership. We will have crossed the finish line, and the fat lady will have sung.

I believe there is more, not as a precondition but simply more for us to consider. Our arrival on the leadership stage is heralded by our delivery with relevance and impact. Reaching that threshold is earned through hard work and the intensity of personal conversations about who we are and what we do. Delivery – OB²T – in partnership with others demonstrates our competence to lead. Opening frontiers of beauty and possibility for life adds meaning and substance. The soldier does not die in vain when the sacrifice is to protect the values of a nation.

There is an extra dimension to awareness when undertaken with a watchful heart. Responses with love and compassion temper the steel of decisions that may of necessity be cold and clinical. Resourcing that searches for challenge rather than cloned compliance and submission adds value beyond measure. Partnering without expedience or selfish expectations takes leadership to a higher level. It matters not whether the fat lady is in tune when she sings as long as she sings the delivery song. There is seldom complete harmony in all that we accomplish as leaders. By its very nature, high-impact leadership will occasionally create turbulence. As the famous Apple Inc. ad states:

> "Here's to the crazy ones, the misfits, the rebels, the troublemakers, the round pegs in the square holes ... the ones who see things differently -- they're not fond of rules, and they have no respect for the status quo. ... You can quote them, disagree with them, glorify or vilify them, but the only thing you can't do is ignore them because they change things. ... They push the human race forward, and while some may see them as the crazy ones, we see genius, because the people who are crazy enough to think that they can change the world, are the ones who do."
>
> "Think Different"
> Apple's advertising campaign, 1997

A VOCABULARY FOR LEADING AND LEADERSHIP

Language is important. The wise choice of words used with small inflections, and sincere emphasis can dramatically influence perceptions. There is always something magnetic about people with a well-developed command of language and fluency of expression. It only comes with plenty of practice.

Abilene Paradox: Why people collectively do what they individually don't want. It gets overcome when the parties involved declare what they want. (From Jerry Harvey.)

Accept: Willingness to go along; buy-in; does not imply agreement.

Accountability: Obligation; on the line for something.

Align: Bringing together – thoughts and ideas.

Apologise: Acknowledgement of an error – something rarely seen in high-profile leaders despite the importance.

Attitude: Disposition towards.

Behaviour: Conduct and actions in response to thoughts feelings, and stimuli from other people.

~~But~~: Banned word.

~~Can't~~: Banned word; replacement: have not yet learnt.

~~Committee~~: Banned word; replacement: task team or working group.

Communicate: Personal, transactional process which attempts to establish shared meaning and/or understanding.

Competence: The overall ability or capability to perform specific tasks and functions successfully.

Competencies: The underlying knowledge, skills, experience, attitudes, habits, routines and well-being that are causally related to successful task completion.

Competent: An adjective to describe someone who can successfully complete specific tasks to an agreed standard.

Converse: Talk; Engage in conversation.

Culture: The sum total of the signs, symbols, rituals, practices, customs and behaviour that shape the unique nature and character of a group, organisation or nation.

Delegation: Responsibilities (work) and commensurate authority assigned to a person, which when understood, and accepted, creates an obligation for performance.

Dialogue: Conversation without judgement; interactions that seek to dissolve rather than resolve differences.

Discipline: Compliance with rules or a code of conduct: a branch of knowledge.

Enrol: To join or get people to join.

Evil: Profoundly immoral and wicked; a quality to be avoided.

Feedback: Information, perspectives and/or assessments given with the intent to assist with self-calibration and change where needed; giving and receiving feedback are highly valued skills.

~~F**k:~~ Complete delete – avoid expletives – they are guttural, not admirable.

Goal: Target; desired outcome.

Great: Popular adjective for meals and movies. Not appropriate for use when referring to leaders.

~~Hate:~~ A toxic feeling; Banned word.

Incompetent: Standard condition for most politicians – fortunately not all – lacking capacity to successfully complete tasks for whcih there is accountability.

Lilies in the Pond: An illustration of exponential growth or decay.

Lead: Be ahead; Take charge; Provide direction.

Leadership: Actions taken to achieve results through the efforts of people.

Learn: Acquisition, distillation, retention and application of knowledge and experience.

Lie: Strictly forbidden.

Mission: Primary objectives; In organisational terms, a statement of primary purpose, products/services, geographic scope, customers/clients and stakeholders.

Objective: Target; desired outcome.

Ownership: Belong to; possession.

Pareto Principle: 80/20; causality of a small amount relative to a large amount or vice versa.

Proficiency: Competence x speed – error.

Responsibility: Work – application of effort and energy to complete tasks.

Role: Combination of tasks typically associated with jobs/positions.

Skill: Ability to do something well/proficiently.

Skilful: Capacity to act automatically and spontaneously with high fluency.

Strategy: Plan and approach to achieve significant outcomes.

Strategic intent: Most important long-term goal/objective.

Structures: Defined in the Oxford Dictionary as 'the arrangement of and relations between the parts or elements of something complex'.

~~**Subordinate**~~: Banned word; replacements: team member, colleague, associate and protégé.

~~**Superior**~~: Banned word; There is no person on the planet who is superior to another. Different – yes; more qualified and experienced – yes; Wiser and wealthier – yes; superior – never; replacements: one-up, supervisor, leader, manager, Head of Department, VP, CEO etc.

Tactical: Intermediate action to achieve an advantage that contributes to the strategy.

Understand: Comprehend.

Values: (Principles) Deeply held beliefs about what is morally right and wrong. Guides for decision-making and behaviour.

Velcro (factor): Two strips of nylon fabric that form a strong bond when pressed together – like team members do when they share goals and values.

Vision: Short emotionally appealing statement of a desired future state/destination.

~~Whistle-blower~~: Unfortunate negative term to describe a person who is courageous enough to expose corrupt practices; Replacements: Informant, activist and principled person.

WAYPOINT 3: MOVING FORWARD: NEXT STEPS

Getting to Carnegie Hall

This story is worth repeating. A visitor to New York heard about Carnegie Hall as a venue where only the best artists in the world perform. Armed with a ticket, he sets out to attend a show only to discover that he has misplaced the address. Sound common sense directs him to ask a rather phased-out-looking character for directions.

"You want to get to Carnegie Hall, Mr?"

"Yes please, Carnegie Hall."

"Carnegie Hall where only the best of the best perform – you want to get there?"

"That's right. How can I get there?"

Clicking his fingers loudly as he points to the visitor: "Practice man, practice. Practice man, practice. That's how you get to join the best of the best. Practice man, practice."

Top achievers know the credo well. They never stop practising, no matter how many life and career changes they make. Professional associations make life-long updating and renewal, mandatory. Couples in lasting relationships, regularly refresh the special moments and memories that first caused them to forge a union. Without reinforcement, knowledge and experience slowly fade into our library of unretrievable assets.

No matter how modest, the greatest value from the time invested in reading this book, will depend on how you use the insights. You can share them, apply them, summarise them, challenge them and even discard them. What you do is your call. But please do something to move forward.

Here are some **suggestions**:

- Select a skill you want to move to a higher level of proficiency and practice it for at least seven iterations or until your goal is achieved. For example, work on 'converging interactions' and 'proper closure'.

- Consciously replace self-defeating and/or degrading words with constructive alternatives. For example, no more 'I can't' becomes 'I have not yet learnt'. Subordinates and superiors are out. There are no such people. Team members, colleagues, my immediate supervisor, my team leader, and best of all, people by name. Make a list and keep it visible.

- Eliminate verbal mannerisms – the repetitive use of superfluous words such as 'like, OK, right, as you know, yes but' and expletives.

- Accelerate and deepen your experience.

- Middle to senior leaders: via sabbaticals, executive courses, network building and visits to 'the fringes' of new and contrarian thinking.

- Young and new leaders: plentiful reading of biographies, 'how to' resources, case studies and multi-cultural leadership publications.

- Get a mentor (we should all have one) who listens, does not judge, is super trustworthy and seeds possibilities.

- Diarise/block time monthly/quarterly for personal reflection and learning: Select aspects of your personal mastery and work on them.

- Create virtuous and enjoyable cycles of regular learning. For example: learn one computer keyboard shortcut a week, one tree or flower a week, one new piece of music or exercise routine a month and one new way of preparing eggs a month – there are 52 options.

- Form a learning group (perhaps several) with friends, and colleagues who are interested in similar topics. Really anything where the members can benefit from shared learning will equate to accelerated learning. Get into a routine and make it fun.

- Get going with your Learning Journal or Life Book.

- Revisit the 'Call to Action' sections.

- Ask for and remain open to feedback from all sources.

- Never ever be defensive or argumentative about feedback no matter how biased or incorrect it may be. Sure, agree to disagree while always making it easy for others to share openly with you.

- Step up and take charge. Lead!

- Practise, man, practise.

RECOMMENDED RESOURCES FOR FURTHER DEVELOPMENT

Understanding and Enjoying Life

David Whyte: **Crossing the Unknown Sea** (Penguin Books: 2001). Short video clips by David Whyte: Plenty on YouTube

Leo Buscaglia: **Personhood: The Art of Being Fully Human** (Ballentine Books: 1978; now hard to source). Video: Only you can make the difference. https://youtube.com/watch?v=wwaKu0U_hqk&feature=shares

Robert Fulghum: **All I Need to Know I Learned in Kindergarten** (Ballantine Books: 2003)

Oxford Union Speakers: Brilliant: Pioneers of Science; Stars of Music, Political Leaders; Sporting Giants; Literary Greats; Stage and Screen first-hand sharing of life experiences as though you are present in the room. Be sure not to miss Stephen Fry, Christopher Hitchens, Richard Dawkins, James Baldwin vs William F Buckley and the legendary Marco Pierre White. http://is.gd/OxfordUnion

I Have a Dream: Martin Luther King https://www.youtube.com/watch?v=3vDWWy4CMhE&t=6s

Commencement Speeches – there are many: Credible advice to students graduating in the USA by mostly credible people. Steve Jobs' Stanford speech is a classic must-view (repeatedly) https://www.youtube.com/watch?v=Hd_ptbiPoXM

Sidney Poitier Receives an Honorary Award: 74th Oscars (2002): https://www.youtube.com/watch?v=mnjTANhBu3k&t=2s

The Marginalian Newsletter – formerly Brain Pickings by Maria Popova: A free weekly jam packed newsletter with lovely life stories with strong roots in poetry, literature, art and activism. Excellent follow through links and references. https://www.themarginalian.org/newsletter

Nobel Prizes: Best of the Best: Acceptance Speeches. https://www.nobelprize.org. Categories according to your interest.

Dire Straits: Sultans of Swing (because life without a love of good music is greatly impoverished) https://www.youtube.com/watch?v=8Pa9x9fZBtY

Ennio Morricone: The Best of Ennio (pure magic especially the Danish National Symphony playing The Good, The Bad and The Ugly) https://www.youtube.com/watch?v=UfcsS0Fwc8U

Samin Nosrat: **Salt, Fat, Acid, Heat: Mastering the Elements of Good Cooking** (Canongate Books, 2017). Also available on Netflix

Learning: The Greatest Means to Abundant Ends

Stephan Reid: **How to Think: Building Your Mental Muscle** (Prentice Hall: 2003)

Atul Gawande: **The Checklist Manifesto: How to Get Things Right** (Profile Books: 2010)

Rolf Dobelli: **The Art of Thinking Clearly** (Sceptre: 2014)

Donella H Meadows: **Thinking in Systems** (Chelsea Green Publishing: 2008)

Nassim Nicholas Taleb: **Antifragile: How to Live in a World We Don't Understand** (Allen Lane: 2012)

Carol C Dweck: **Mindset: The New Psychology of Success** (Ballantine Books: 2006)

Leonard Mlodinow: **The Drunkard's Walk: How Randomness Rules Our Lives** (Penguin Books: 2009)

Michael J Mauboussin: **Think Twice: Harnessing the Power of Counterintuition** (Harvard Business School Press: 2009)

Sir Ken Robinson (on TED):
- Do schools kill creativity? (Posted Jun 2006)
- Bring on the learning revolution! (Posted May 2010)
- How to escape education's death valley (Posted May 2013)
- Sir Ken Robinson (still) wants an education revolution (Posted Dec 2018)

Leading and Leadership

Ray Dalio: **Principles** (Simon and Schuster: 2017)

Adam Grant: **Think Again: The Power of Knowing What You Don't Know** (Penguin Random House: 2021)

Reed Hastings and *Erin Meyer*: **No Rules Rules: Netflix and the Culture of Reinvention** (Penguin Random House: 2020)

Tom Peters: **The Little Big Things: 163 Ways to Pursue Excellence** (HarperCollins: 2010)

Mikael Krogerus and *Roman Tschäppeler*: **The Decision Book: Fifty Models for Strategic Thinking** (Profile Books: 2008)

Chip and *Dan Heath*: **Made to Stick: Why some ideas take hold and others come unstuck** (rhBooks: 2007)

Max DePree: **Leadership is an Art** (Dell Paperback: 1989)

Geoff Garrett and *Graeme Davies*: **Herding Cats: Being advice to aspiring academic and research leaders** (Tiarchypress: 2010)

Films and documentaries

Robin Williams: **Dead Poets Society**

Gene Hackman and Denzel Washington: **Crimson Tide**

Meryl Streep, Anne Hathaway and Emily Blunt: **The Devil Wears Prada**

Al Pacino: **Scent of a Woman** – especially the School Tribunal scene towards the end of the film

Julia Roberts: **Erin Brockovich**

Tom Cruise and Jack Nicholson: **A Few Good Men**

Daniel Day-Lewis: **Lincoln**

THANKS

Leaders say thank you, and they say it often. What they achieve requires the help of others. I am grateful from the core of my being, for the distilled insights, learning and experiences gathered directly and indirectly, over my lifetime, from leaders, clients, students, academics, authors, scientists, colleagues, friends, family and critics across the globe. Thank you one and all.

There are simply too many people to list them all here. As a token of respect and appreciation, I have named a few who have left lasting memories, and I apologise to the many I have of necessity had to omit.

Direct in-person influence, support and help:

JUMBO JURGENS: *Junior school teacher*

NICK SEDDAN: *English teacher*

DI DOMS: *School parent*

DOREEN ANN: *My mom*

PJG DE VOS (VLAKKIES): *The man who lifted me from the crowd*

OCKERT SNYMAN: *RSM Military Academy*

BEN BENADE: *OI: Military Academy*

MAGNUS MALAN: *Chief of the Defence Force, the finest leader served*

JAN VAN LOGGERENBERG: *OC: Military Academy*

CHRIS VAN ZYL: *Life-long comrade in arms*

NEVIL J HERMER: *Role model boss*

HOWARD COOK: *Role model boss*

ANDREW JENNINGS: *Colleague and courageous client*

BRAIN CLARK: *International CEO role model and pace-setter*

GEOFFREY GARRETT: *Client, role model and 911 friend*

JANET GARRETT: *Model mother, partner and leader*

NAMANE MAGAU: *Client and mentor*

PETRO TERBLANCHE: *Pace-setter and model learner*

TINA EBOKA: *Role model super achiever*

JOHANN AHLERS: *Client, passionate leader and special friend*

PIET STEYN: *Client, friend and scientist extraordinaire*

GUNER GURTUNCA: *Client and friend*

WYNAND MARX (BUURMAN): *Client, mega leader and friend extraordinaire*

JOCHEN SCHWEITZER: *Client and friend*

HENNIE DU PLESSIS: *Trusted colleague and leader*

WESSEL DU PREEZ (BUDDY): *Buddy x10 says it all*

RENE RING: *Exemplary PA and 911 friend*

LESLEY WRIGHT: *Exemplary PA and mega organiser*

NARESH KUMAR: *Client and life-long friend*

RAMESH MASHELKAR: *Client and global role model*

HIRO BHOJWANI (SILVER FOX): *My Indian mentor*

SAXY SAXENA: *Student, client and life-long friend*

DAN AMLALO: *Brave pioneering leader and colleague*

EHRLICH DESA: *Harshest critic and trusted friend*

P S RAJINI: *Student, tutor and comrade*

ANDRÉ MORGENTHAL: *My catalytic gusty-bush friend*

ISABELLA SUSANNA DEAN: *Loving wife*

MARISA BRACHER: *Inspiring daughter*

ADRIAN DEAN: *#2/3 – A role model son*

NORÉNE DEAN: *Once a wife; Now a sister; Always a friend*

DAVID CAROLUS: *Client and effervescent leader*

DIXON WARUNGE: *Client and man of few words*

DIANE RITSON: *My 'Fireball' 911 Counsellor*

Indirect influence through their work:

NELSON MANDELA: *A national hero and global role model*

LEO BUSCAGLIA: *We never met but the example he set triggered mega change in my life*

WARREN BENNIS: *Author and leadership guru*

TOM PETERS: *Author, consultant and agent provocateur*

RUSSEL ACKHOFF: *Author and thought leader par excellence*

DAVID WHYTE: *Poet, agent of life and inspirer*

RICHARD FEYNMAN: *Brilliant scientist and teacher*

DANIEL KAHNEMAN: *Mind-blowing thinker and teacher*

DANIEL QUINN: *Author – Ishmael; A visit to humanity*

STEVE JOBS: *World leader decades ahead of his time*

WILLIAM H McRAVEN: *Character carved service*

ALAN FLETCHER: *Creative, inspiring genius*

LIZ CHENEY: *Modern-day Joan of Arc*

TREVOR NOAH: *Born a sin; Evolved to iconic model of achievement*

ROBERT FULGHUM: *Inspiring author on life*

Special thanks:

JOHANN AHLERS and PIET STEYN *for all their encouragement, support and hard work to ensure this book was completed.*

INDEX

A

ActionPlan Sample 154

Analytical tools for environmental scanning 146

Authority
 Other 65
 Personal 56, 59-64, 69
 Positional 56-59, 62

C

Challenger, Space Shuttle Disaster 16

Checklist for Leading and Leadership 33

Chinese Rice Farmers 95

Competence
 Crafting your framework 83
 Deciding what matters most 97
 Frameworks – Examples 83
 Functional 93
 Generic 83
 Parts of 71
 Personal
  Importance of 101
  Personal Mastery – as cornerstone for leading and life 97
 Role in leadership 173

Compound interest: Formula 116

Credibility: Primary foundations 63

D

Du Preez, Wessel
 My Twiddly Bits for Hollandaise Sauce 79
 On Rolf Dobelli 30, 92

H

Habits and routines 71, 101, 124-125, 128, 137

I

Identity 17, 23, 36-37, 43, 85, 93, 98, 107, 119, 133-135

Influence: Types and sources 56

K

Knopfler, Mark: Sultans of Swing 77-78

L

Leadership
 Defined 17, 29, 51, 57, 59, 70, 140, 186
 Expanded definition 54
 Holy Grail 150-151, 179
 Vocabulary 183
 Work (roles)
  Awareness 146
  Delivery 171
  Learning 172
  Partnering 163, 167, 169
  Resourcing 160
  Responses 150, 158

Leading
 Explained 42, 140
 Multiple interpretations 44
 Test 33, 36, 40, 85, 108-109, 128, 143, 161
 Test suggested answers 40

M

Mindsets
　As structure driving behaviour and results　102
　Evolving Paradigms　104
　Key features　102
　Modelling　133
Modelling and change
　Behaviours　109
　Skills　109
Moving Forward, Some Options　32
Moving Forward: Next Steps　188

P

Personal Mastery
　Actions to develop　136
　As a cornerstone　97, 109
　Attitudes　118
　Behaviours　109
　Experience　129
　Habits and routines　124
　Leverage for change　106
　Unpacked　99
　Values　118

Planner – Weekly　126, 127
Principle, Pareto　83, 125, 185
Proficiency defined and illustrated　79
Purpose: Of this book　41

R

Resources for further development　191

T

Trust: The Gold Standard　65-66

V

Values and attitudes　118, 123

W

What we think we know – Sinking of the Titanic　27
Who am 'I'　133-134
Work as Meaning and Identity　93

Author's Information

Ian Dean has spent over 45 years in the leader and people development domain. Having interacted with thousands of people from 57 cultures, he has learnt the value of diversity and why and how being able to lead is an essential life skill for everybody. For him, people who cannot lead are no better off than people who cannot read. He places greater value on a capacity to provide pragmatic leadership than fluency in theories and models. He regards the life-long quest for personal mastery as the integrating force for personal and leadership growth.